Rediscover

Humaira Nasim

Rediscover
Copyright © 2020 Humaira Nasim
First published in 2020

ISBN
Paperback: 978-0-6486663-3-2
E-book: 978-0-6486663-5-6

All rights reserved. No part of this book may be reproduced, stored in a retrieval system, or transmitted by any means (electronic, mechanical, photocopying, recording, or otherwise) without written permission from the author.

Because of the dynamic nature of the Internet, any web addresses or links contained in this book may have changed since publication and may no longer be valid. The information in this book is based on the author's experiences and opinions. The views expressed in this book are solely those of the author and do not necessarily reflect the views of the publisher; the publisher hereby disclaims any responsibility for them.

The author of this book does not dispense any form of medical, legal, financial, or technical advice either directly or indirectly. The intent of the author is solely to provide information of a general nature to help you in your quest for personal development and growth. In the event you use any of the information in this book, the author and the publisher assume no responsibility for your actions. If any form of expert assistance is required, the services of a competent professional should be sought.

Publishing information
Publishing, design, and production facilitated by
Passionpreneur Publishing
www.PassionpreneurPublishing.com

Melbourne, VIC | Australia

Dedication

In the loving memory of my grandmother, Zubaida Khatoon.
The iron lady who often hugs me in my dreams.

Foreword

سلسلۂ روز و شب، سازِ ازل کی فغاں
جس سے دکھاتی ہے ذاتِ زیر و بم ممکنات

'The succession of day and night is the reverberation of the symphony of Creation.

Through its modulations, the Infinite demonstrates the parameters of possibilities.'

— Allama Muhammad Iqbal

Testimonials

'One of the things I love about Humaira is her realistic, no-nonsense approach to personal change. Despite being a wonderfully warm, kind and patient person, she knows that change does not come about by simply sitting around hoping for it, and instead knows that a success-mindset, coupled with action, will empower us to create the results we want to see. Having had the pleasure of getting to know Humaira as she embarked on her own personal and professional journey, I know she is a coach who supports her clients wholly on their own paths to personal discovery.'

Linda Bonnar
Master NLP Coach and Practitioner, Author and Trainer.

'Humaira, so passionately, tackles one of the most important questions in life, our relationship with life! If you are ready to rediscover yourself then Humaira surely can help.'

Moustafa Hamwi
The Passionpreneur

'Humaira has touched some sensitive issues of our Asian society through this book. It is an eye-opener and a much needed guide for many. In these changing times, this book is a trendsetter and a first step in the long journey of human self-rediscovery, especially in South Asia.

The author has kept the language simple and straight forward. Each chapter uniquely touches the heart and mind, and the reader makes their own journey of self-rediscovery.'

Eram Khan
Early Years and Montessori Expert

Table of Contents

Prologue	The City That Never Sleeps	xi
Chapter One	The Power of Intention	1
Chapter Two	Grandma's Pink Shoes	15
Chapter Three	Leaky Boundaries	27
Chapter Four	I Love Being Naked	43
Chapter Five	Tick-Tock Goes the Clock	59
Chapter Six	The Motivational Fuel	71
Chapter Seven	Striking Balance	83
Chapter Eight	The Invincible You	97
Chapter Nine	Beyond Negative Space	107
Chapter Ten	The Science of the Seen and the Signs of the Unseen	119
Chapter Eleven	The Secret to Abundance	131
Chapter Twelve	Amplify Your Influence	143
Chapter Thirteen	Unleash Success	151
Epilogue	The Circle of Life	167

Prologue

The City That Never Sleeps

It was the summer of 2018, and I was standing at the Mount of Light (*Jabal an-Nūr*). Many thoughts that had been racing in my head had suddenly come to a standstill. I could feel the serenity and peace that this place had always been known for.

I and my husband on our return from Mina, having completed the holy ritual of Hajj, had planned to hike the mountain and visit the cave of Hira later in the night. It was known that this Mount is miraculously lit even at night so climbing up even in the dark would be easy. And yes, so it was. Standing gracefully amidst all other mountains, this mountain could easily be recognized from a distance and hence the name. There was something about this place and the entire city. My heart was feeling a magnetic pull towards it. We headed towards the cave and offered the voluntary prayers.

We spent the whole night at the mountain top. Honestly, when viewing the city from the top, there was nothing much that could attract my senses but the silence in the air had its own rhythm. I wished I had a container or a bottle in which I could fill all the peace and tranquillity of this place and take back home. I wanted to pour it drop by drop on to every memory of mine that disrupted my peace and on to the uncertain future that increased my anxiety. To use this magic potion to answer the questions that kept on lingering in my mind. Pouring on to the experiences that had rubbed me, thanking them for the learning and insights they enriched me with and on to the experiences that overjoyed me giving me patience and strength to hold on tight; both of them together giving a meaningful existence to my life. The only thing that was possible was to live in the moment. Even if I had tried reminiscing through my past or planning my future, the charm of Makkah would never let me do so . . . .

I decided to make memories instead, to make them an anchor to *REDISCOVER* myself. To soak as much of the peace as I could of the glorious history this city has witnessed.

Chapter One

The Power of Intention

Have you ever wondered what lies at the root of any action? Have you ever questioned why you do things the way you do? What is the underlying motive or agenda behind your actions? Or like everyone else, does your life run on autopilot, like a robot programmed through environmental conditioning? Have social boundaries and fears trained you to follow certain routines, hold certain beliefs and own certain values?

Human beings educate themselves through social learning. In order to make learning easier, we have a natural tendency to learn from other people's experiences. This is a great and intelligent approach as long as we do not pacify the element of curiosity and questioning by following them blindly. When we follow suit without questioning, we overlook the fact that the time and space in which these other people had their experiences were different from ours. The moment we stop questioning the WHY behind any action, we start losing the essence of that action so much so that generations pass and we don't realise that we have been following rituals that make no sense in this time and era, but we do it because our forefathers did it.

In this chapter, I would like to discuss the missing element that brings energy and power into your actions and leads to the desired outcome, an often neglected concept: intention.

> *Intention can be defined as the thought generating a gush of energy, positive or negative associated with any action. The kind of energy that flows with each action determines the success or loss accompanying it.*

The Importance of Intention

Intentions drive motivation, and motivation is the driving force behind action.

Interestingly, even if you don't consciously know the reasons behind your actions, your subconscious knows your motives. It's just that you have forgotten to question it to bring it into your awareness. The habits that you form work on the same principle. When you start brushing your teeth twice a day with an intention to have good oral hygiene and repeat the habit multiple times, your brain learns this pattern. It is wired a certain way, and your intention and purpose go in the background. Your brain starts running on an algorithm whose output is cleaner teeth. Just imagine what will happen if your brain learns an algorithm like sitting for hours in a posture that could affect your spine. What if this turns into an everyday norm? What output would this algorithm generate? It is for this reason that bad habits are so lethal. And it is for this very reason that you should bring mindfulness into your actions by consciously making an intention. By now it should be clear why bringing intentions into your awareness is extremely important.

Having said this, if the brain has to process the intention each and every time, it may get too tired. Therefore, it is equally important to form good habits that could let your 24/7, 365-day working brain rest for a bit. At the same time, you should be re-evaluating and reforming these habits whenever the need arises. This will break the routine and ensure you are not following a pattern out of mere habit and no need.

Even habitual prayers and worship lose their essence; that is why the mind that inherently cannot remain still starts wandering elsewhere during prayers, because it is not mindful and conscious of the habitual bodily actions and lip movements. Therefore, you do not experience the ultimate benefit of prayers and worship. Instead of bringing ease into your life, they become a burden.

Intentions can be positive or negative; they control your actions. Intentions that carry positive energy generate the right results. No matter how good an action seems to be, it is only defined by its intention and in the long run proves the power of intention. Often, you perform good actions, but you have a secret agenda – a cause that serves another purpose than the action performed. Nevertheless, you get the outcome based on your intention. If you help others in order to get recognised and appreciated in your circle, the power of intention is so strong that now or later you will get ridiculed at the hands of the same people in whose eyes you had sought appreciation in the first place.

Identify Your Intentions

Sometimes intentions are well wrapped, making it difficult for you to identify them. In fact, you may be quick in judging the actions of others than your own. Consider this scenario:

Two siblings are in a room fighting over a toy that belongs to one of them who does not want to share.

The first one argues, 'I share my toys, but he or she never does and is so selfish'.

How would you resolve this situation?

To the child who shares his toys, ask the question: *Why do you share?* Most likely, he will say, *Because sharing is good.* Ask him again: *Why do you think sharing is good?* If he replies, *Because then we can play together,* ask him: *Do you like to play with others?* If he says, *Yes I love playing with others,* reiterate his answers: *So you share because you love playing together and you need company, which means are you SELFISH?* The child might also answer: *I share as it's a good bargain; I give my things, and in return he shares his.* Ask him, *Are you interested in other people's things? Are you not satisfied with your own? Do you share because you are GREEDY?* To the child who doesn't want to share, ask: *Why don't you share?* He will say, *because I want to play by myself.* You can ask: *So, you don't like to play with others?* He will most likely say *no.* And he will most likely not be interested in the belongings of others, as he is satisfied with his own things. *Then why do you take the toys of the other child?* The child may say: *Because he gives me and asks me to play with him.* Reiterate the child's answers by asking him: *You don't want to share because you think you are SELF-SUFFICIENT? And you don't share because you don't like playing together, which means that there is a personal motive and you are SELFISH too?*

The truth is all human beings are selfish, but unfortunately, they are quick to label each other and judge their intentions. Your actions may appear selfless, but they are not altruistic at all. You cater to your own desires and needs, but to the world you present yourself as the most generous human being. Hence, it is necessary to ask yourself the WHY question, to keep checking on your intentions. Because actions without the right intentions can fool the world, but the energies associated with them never die. It is very important to regularly ask yourselves what you do and why you do it. This way, you will have clarity of the motives behind your actions; it will be easier for you to know yourself, your needs and desires, and satisfy them in better ways; and you will avoid manipulating people and situations for your personal gains and not let others do the same to you.

So how would you resolve the above sibling fight so that they can peacefully coexist? What is the middle ground where it's a win-win for both kids, and neither has to compromise their personal needs nor be insensitive to the other's needs? The understanding of the balance between self-care and fulfilling others' needs wherein both are acts of *sadaqa* (charity) will help them identify the right intentions without labelling each other through self-serving biases.

Humans are selfish by nature. They work on self-serving motives. However, a person's stature is determined by what kind of motives they work for. Certainly, these motives provide him with something: some people engage in charity to gain appreciation, others do to gain contentment and happiness, but all of them are getting something out of that same act. Humans are not *As-Samad* (The Self-Sufficient). They are needy, selfish creations. Their intentions define their motives. Neither can you judge the intentions of others, nor do you know their intentions. Whatever their intentions might be, they will serve the human being's purpose in this life or in the next, depending on their values and beliefs. Either for them or against them.

Maximise Your Gains by Making the Right and Purest Intentions

It is very important to raise kids with the right intentions. As parents, you should not look for a bargain lesser than what you deserve for carrying out this noble responsibility. Drawing the boundaries of expectations around your kids, especially sons, as a return of your sacrifices you did for them is a very cheap return to look forward to or even intend in the first place while raising them. Reliance on children and treating them as your worldly investment often leads to unfulfilled expectations as well as a crippling relationship between them and you. It is filled with regrets, complaints and conflicts that could deter peaceful coexistence or, to another extreme, that could suck your children's energy in pleasing you and meeting your expectations and wishes. If you treat them as an investment for the afterlife, you're creating the right intention of raising them with the values that will not let them abandon you in the first place as well as giving them space to evolve rather than being bound by fear or caged with the limits you set for them. This will also liberate you from the constant fear, insecurity and power struggle that compel you to keep them holding tightly. Consequently, through their unlimited and unbarred accomplishments, they will make you proud both in this world and hereafter. So, the next time your child has dreams, believe in him and let him discover his own path.

As parents, it is your responsibility to work on driving the right motivation behind your children's actions. For example, a child who is offered goodies in exchange for good actions and behaviours tends to become a trader, exchanging good behaviours for something in return. Children should be taught integrity and personal values, which will go a long way rather than the temporary rewards that may compel them to do an action with the wrong intention. In the absence of rewards, they may fall back on old behaviours. However, it is part of human nature to expect rewards in exchange for their efforts especially when they must work against their ego and desires. In order to channelise natural instincts, there is an effective way to resolve and maintain a balance.

Usually when you – as a parent – take power and authority in your hands, it is quite unlikely that you fit the picture of a role model and an embodiment of perfection to direct the kids to follow you. When they find an incongruency in your behaviour, which is occasionally present (as part of human imperfection), they will stop respecting you. When you shift the power and authority to a Being that is Absolute, Perfect and has power over His Dominion and is not limited by human needs and desires, it will be easier to maintain that equilibrium where accountability of the family shifts to the Higher power than on you, while everyone is held equally accountable based on the rights and responsibilities defined by the divine law.

You should avoid rewarding for actions ordained by Allah for its reward lies with Him alone.

For example, charity events that are meant to support the less privileged of society are backed by their own marketing agendas. Under the umbrella of good action, businesses want to promote and market themselves. For example, take charity events where you get an instant return like a charity dinner or a concert that gives you instant gratification in the form of either satisfying your taste buds or providing you entertainment. You are deprived of the soulful experience that charity claims to provide, that is, reducing your own burdens and stresses of life by serving others in need. The reward of charity – delayed gratification – builds strength and self-control and helps build your character as you sacrifice an asset, be it time, effort or money. These soulful rewards are usually absent in such marketing events.

I realised this when my nine-year-old daughter told me about a charity game that was to be held at her school. The idea was to contribute money to an orphanage and enjoy a fun game in return. I couldn't grasp the idea, as I found that the element of sacrifice and attitude of *giving* was entirely missing. It was instant gratification: What am I getting in return and what is the ROI? This might be a very small matter, but in the larger scheme of things, it takes away the benefits of delayed gratification of being rewarded in the afterlife as well as our reliance on God.

The intention should be to help the other person and not to trade for your service. Yes, humans are not unconditional beings and do look after their self-interest, but something that is done in the name of social service should remain as such and not lose its soul. I am not saying that this model of instant gratification does not serve the needy, but it does not serve your soul. There is no harm in such a collaboration but it should be with an entirely different name and entirely different gains and not under the banner of charity. Charity should be solely a business between you and your Lord.

Your actions carry the energies of your intention; hence, people can feel this energy. If you have pure intentions, your presence brings peace in the surroundings and you reflect a light of genuineness and authenticity. You radiate vibrance and harmony and project the same onto the people in your surroundings. People start loving you and cherish your company because they feel good and uplifted in your presence.

On the other hand, ill intentions, no matter how good your actions apparently are, carry negative energy, which is also projected onto your surroundings. Your superficial actions fail to cover up, and people feel discomfort in your presence. They start avoiding you and perceive you as a negative person.

Intention defines our purpose, and the bigger the purpose, the more meaningful and impactful our life becomes. Interestingly, when we intend for a greater cause and purpose, all little gains come as by-products. Let me explain with an example: When I would wake my kids up for *Fajr*, I made sure that their intention to wake up and pray is only to please Allah. They should not pray because I ask them to or to receive a reward from me, but instead solely to fulfil their personal responsibility and commitment towards their Creator. If the intention is anything other than this, the kids would lose the essence and benefit of the worship they do so diligently. In summers, since the days are longer, the sunrise would be earlier. There would be enough time for a short nap before the kids had to leave for school. However, waking them up was more difficult as the nights would be relatively shorter. So when I woke them up for prayers, I would tell them to get up early so they had ample time to sleep again before they had to wake up again for school. The total time for sleep actually stayed the same, but just the thought of getting a chance to go back to sleep was alluring to their tired bodies and a very good incentive for them. As a result, they would wake up immediately with the intention to finish their prayers as fast as they can, so they could jump back into bed and snuggle with their pillows. My mission to wake them up was successful, but did I help them benefit from the prayers offered in a rush or was it just a ritual to mark attendance? What if they could have a higher intention of waking up early in servitude to God, so as to please Him more and attain His blessings? It would definitely make them more mindful of their prayers, still giving them ample time for a nap before school. Thus, higher intentions automatically encompass the little ones within them. They help in getting the most benefit out of actions, including the lesser gains, while at the same time not losing the essence of those actions.

'Don't waste your actions; make the best intentions.'

Another common example from South Asian culture is young girls who face social pressure to look good and thus create the intention of maintaining a healthy body in order to get good proposals. Because their intention is short-lived, their motivation generally ends once they get married and they may gain weight to the point of obesity. Creating the intention of fulfilling the rights of your body and expressing gratitude to God for giving you a healthy body can be far more beneficial to help amplify your gain. The action will be long-lived, leaving a prolonged impact on your health and well-being while at the same time including the shorter-lived and lesser gains.

Acquiring education is a process and a continuous learning. When it is limited to being a means of earning bread and butter, your intention becomes limited and you can only reach what you had aimed for. Your intention may be as small as having a house, a family, a car or it could be as big as serving the world and contributing to make it a better place. With this intention, you should think of what problems you can solve by discovering your talents that can help in finding their solutions. Thus, your aim to acquire education should not limit you to select the fields that have the greatest scope and money, but instead, you should create opportunities around your own interests. And with that, the smaller gains of having a house, a family and a car are also achieved along the way.

'Intentions define your destiny.'

A person's success lies in finding a bigger purpose for his actions. The bigger the WHY behind your actions, the more you will transcend as a human being.

You can't make intentions on behalf of other people, so make sure whatever you intend is your own inner calling. You cannot intend to make someone quit smoking unless he intends to do so – that is, you can't help someone who does not want to help himself.

Don't borrow an intention. Don't become a doctor because your parents intended to make you one. Otherwise, your intention will be to please them rather than be a doctor. Hence you won't ever shine as one.

Power of Words
Intentions are powered by words that miraculously turn intentions into actions. They are the bridge of communication between the soul and the body. So, if you want to turn your intentions into reality, words can help you do so.

Back in the days when there was no technology, there was a man who found it difficult to wake up early morning for his morning prayer. Every time he woke up, the sun would be shining on his face. Missing his morning prayer made him sad. He discovered a technique that actually worked for him. He would say action words to himself before going to bed: 'I will wake up at dawn.' He would repeat this mantra multiple times before falling asleep. Surprisingly, he did wake up at dawn. This proves the power of words. They were *words* that influenced the people of Arab fourteen years ago and shaped the history of the world. Positive words give rise to positive thoughts and transform you positively, while negative words like criticism and curses have the power to demotivate you. *Doas* (supplications) are power capsules that motivate you to keep going.

So that your intentions produce the outcome, you should have action words posted on your office desk, on your fridge, on your Facebook wall or any place where you spend the most time. Make sure you change their position as well as the wordings often, or else they won't capture your attention for long.

What if my good intentions are overridden by bad intentions?

When you start doing something, especially a social service with a good intention, somewhere in the middle your thoughts may wander and you lose your 'Why'. For example, you may think, *When my next-door neighbour Saeed will see me feeding orphans and will mention my service in the neighbourhood, I will be known as a philanthropist.* The desire of being recognised as a philanthropist will compel you to take action, like increasing your visibility while doing similar acts of social service, thereby playing on your good intentions in the subtlest manner.

Check whether your actions have good intentions or are for ego satisfaction, because if you nurture your ego through your actions it will only keep growing, turning you into a narcissist. Hence, it is essential that when someone else appreciates you, you don't internalise their compliments. Or else it will rob you of the right motivation and you will fall into a pit of self-love.

What if my actions are sincere, but they produce unfavourable actions or mistakes?
The positive energy associated with your sincerest intentions never go waste and is manifested in ways you can never imagine. Even if you fail at delivering the outcome you had imagined, your efforts will not go waste and you will get the deserved outcome in forms that you may not even know. At the same time, those mistakes could actually be the best outcomes. How? Mistakes are lessons, the stepping stones to future success.

What if people judge my intentions?
Your intention is always between you and your Lord. People can keep guessing or spotting your brain patterns, but it is impossible to be 100% sure of someone's true intention. Don't lose focus by giving explanations. Just keep going.

What if people question my intention and my acts are seemingly unacceptable for the people around me, but I have an intuitive feeling of satisfaction?
Inner contentment, your *fitrah* (natural disposition) and your connection with your Lord stand supreme. As long as your actions are not punishable by law or harmful to others, they are okay. You may have the perception and understanding that others may not be aware of.

Having said so, your intentions get conditioned as you grow up, because of the social pressures and fears that you live with and the expectations that you are bound to meet. In the next chapters, you will identify the factors that corrupt your intention and learn to overcome them to the best of your ability.

Summary

- Don't follow the crowd; be curious enough to find out the reasons behind your actions.
- Before aiming to do something, identify the WHY? Check if that is powerful and beneficial enough to have multiple gains without losing the essence of your actions.
- Start your action in the name of Allah. This will help you bring mindfulness in your work while at the same time ensure that your actions will be supported by the one who is the Most Compassionate and the Most Merciful, who will overlook all your weaknesses and shortcomings. By calling upon the Power of heavens and the earth, you will unleash your own potential and ability through Him.
- Don't make the mistake of judging the intentions of others.

Chapter Two

Grandma's Pink Shoes

The biggest challenge you may face when treading on the path of self-discovery is shedding off the layers and layers of conditioning covering your soul to the extent that even its tiniest shriek is unheard. These layers may be handed to you by your childhood associations, projections by your parents and teachers, and socialisation with your peers and culture in which you are raised.

Social pressure is giving in to the values of anything other than your own, which are not accepted within you. It is the invisible fence that limits your thinking and potential to look beyond the social norms and ideals. The moment you cross the fence, you are bashed by society, laughed upon and cast out.

The moment you break the shackles of social expectations, you become a free person. You are the decision maker of your life, and nobody else can rule over it. You discover your own path rather than walking on the one laid by socially constructed ideals. The question then arises, how can you break these shackles that limit your freedom?

The Loop of Family Expectations

In our society, boys are expected not to cry. Their emotions are often ignored and suppressed from childhood; society makes them feel embarrassed whenever they try to express their feelings. As a result, when emotions don't have an outlet, they get accumulated in the form of aggression and anger. This world does not need angry young men. It needs genuine, compassionate and emotional boys who have the permission to vent their frustrations so that their passions don't die. They should be told that it is okay to cry instead of polishing their ego.They try to portray themselves as macho yet are emotionally brittle humans from inside. Boys are expected to keep their passions and dreams aside in order to financially support their family who have sacrificed a lot in raising them. With this burden on his shoulders, a boy heads for a college education not to pursue what he desires but to attain an education that would secure him a job, make him financially stable to build a house, run the household, fulfil his parents' unrealised dreams and marry a girl of their choice to start his family.

Once society produces this robotic and the most eligible bachelor in town, the hunt for the ideal wife begins. In order to fit into the "ideal girl" vision, girls are trained from childhood to follow socially defined norms, compromise their own passions and desires and become a people pleaser. It is for this reason that a strong-headed woman with ambitions of her own is highly disliked as she may tame the son of this society, which has put so much effort to raise and condition him in a certain way. Girls are expected to help out in household chores, while boys are pampered. Not only should girls be excellent in housekeeping, but they should also be outstanding students and hold professional degrees. And of course, the cherry on the top for the ideal candidate for this highly eligible bachelor is that she should be fair complexioned, tall and have the perfect figure.

Not only are girls faced with the pressure to get married, but also to do so at the right age – whatever that might be – not when they are ready to enter a relationship, and then, are expected to give their best to keep the relationship going. This is a lot for young girls to bear. How do they find the time to reflect and discover their true selves? The girls, contradictory to the boys, are emotion bombs who, when left with no choice, may start venting the negativity trapped inside and develop a victim mentality.

I don't wish to delve into the details of this hunt, which itself is very heartbreaking and scary. Finally, when Cinderella whose foot fits the glass shoe is found, the nuptials begin.

Weddings in our culture are another extravaganza. You are expected to spend a fortune of your life's hard-earned money. Your dreams revolve around having to accumulate enough wealth so as to marry your kids in the most pompous way. On the contrary, simplicity can bring so much ease and release people from this undue pressure. This energy and money can then be utilised to find their true passions and fulfil a higher purpose instead of holding a large feast to impress others and feeling accepted by society. This is true especially nowadays when celebrations are not limited to just a single day, but to pre-and post-marriage functions. People indulge in such ostentatious shows to remain part of the society or else they will be outcasted.

As the newlyweds belonging to entirely different backgrounds, upbringing, likes and dislikes are adjusting to their new lives amidst the teething chaos, certain inquisitive people in society do not spare them from popping question like *when are you giving us good news* – which translates as when are they planning a baby. Thus, the will to start a family is also dictated to the couple, let alone the choice of raising their kids the way they want.

The newlyweds go through a rollercoaster ride, being pulled from all sides. The daughter-in-law is expected to have excellent manners as per the traditions and values of the new family she has just become a part of, while the poor husband starts losing hair from the stress to maintain a balance between his mother and wife. For the girl, on the other hand, the doors to her old home are closed and she is left at the mercy of new tides in which she must learn to swim. She is exploited under the name of patience and tolerance to bear all kinds of attitudes and behaviours from her in-laws. Under such circumstances, when a child is born, he not only sparks joy for the parents but he also ignites their unfulfilled dreams and desires. These dreams are placed on his shoulders with the very first breath he takes. No wonder the cry! Thus, with these projections, the loop of social expectations begins.

> *'A mother with suppressed and negative emotions can only raise a child who has a negative mind, and thus the same adult will enter the society.'*

When the parents who put so much energy and money into raising their son now see him busy with his own family and work, it breaks their heart, especially the mother's. Her kids have always been her life's focus, as she neglected taking care of herself, or discovering and pursuing her passion. She finds it difficult to empty her nest; hence she doesn't give her children the wings to fly. Her children become her only asset – an investment she is unwilling to let go at any cost.

In a society where sons are the most sought, just imagine the plight of parents who don't have one. Not to mention the pressure on single mothers, the not-so-attractive girls, the overaged, the divorcee who did not give in to societal pressure, the widows, the girls with special needs, those who were sexually abused or the less privileged of our society – who is going to marry them if they don't fit the picture of an ideal candidate for the sons of society? Does society have a sustainable plan for them without quelling their natural desires or are parents willing to marry their sons to not-so-ideal girls or is polygamy the solution? If it's none of the above, then what answers do we have for the chants of uprising feminism, because then they are right – marriage is not the destination. I leave this for you as food for thought.

Materialism, Peer Pressure and Social Comparisons

There was a 10-year-old boy whose school trainers were not fitting him anymore. His parents were having a busy week and had promised to get him a new pair on the weekend. Three days were still left for the week to end, and his shoes were too uncomfortable for him to spend the whole day wearing them. The next morning, he decided to wear his Grandma's shoes till he would get his own, since they both wore the same size of shoes. Her pair of trainers were white with pink laces. He did not have the slightest idea of what he may face at school. In fact, he was quite happy and excited to wear his Grandma's shoes. However, his mother knew what would happen. To prepare him for the bullying that he would face at school, she kissed him on his cheeks while dropping him at the school gate, advising him firmly:

'Become a trendsetter, make it your style.'

When he returned from school in the afternoon, he told his mum that he did not want to wear the pink shoes.

'At no cost will I ever wear these pink shoes again.'

A child who, a few hours ago, so happily and lovingly wore his grandmother's shoes now had become extremely reluctant to do so. This simple story depicts how social/peer pressure can influence your likes and dislikes, and how you can become slaves to the demands and wishes of society at large – letting go off your own desires and associations.

The child's mother had found the right opportunity to teach him a valuable life lesson. She told him that this situation would keep repeating itself unless he learned the lesson. The sooner he did, the easier it would be for him to break the shackles of social pressure. As he grows up, it will be more challenging to break free from this pressure and will be difficult for him to handle it at that time.

She asked him to visualise in his mind's eye three versions of himself and gave him three choices. The first picture was of him having not learnt the lesson, wanting to go to the mall right now – becoming the slave of his peers and giving in to their bullying – and buying new shoes. The second picture was of him having understood the lesson but not willing to learn it, and therefore letting the situation repeat eventually, in much harder ways. He was not willing to wear the pink shoes and instead would continue to wear his old tight shoes – giving in to the social reactions at the cost of hurting his feet. And finally, there is the third picture of himself, one who has learnt the lesson. He will wear the pink shoes the following day as well and proudly show them off if anyone tries to bully him for his choice.

The boy who was by then calmer and had overcome the harsh comments of his peers chose the third version and went to school the following day wearing the same pink shoes. His mother had packed him his favourite lunch so that it would elevate his mood in case he faced any bullying. When he returned from school, his mother asked: 'How was your day?' to which he responded, 'Oh the lunch was great!' – which meant that any discomfort or disturbance related to the pink shoes disappeared to the point that he did not even remember the issue and it was just another good day for him.

Child rearing is also not spared from social pressure. There are many challenges that parents have to face while raising their kids. Materialism tops this list; teaching kids about gratitude and self-control becomes the biggest challenge. You see their peers boasting about their new video game and the latest gadget. Raising your kids with a value system that is opposite to the latest trends becomes quite challenging.

Social norms define the ideals and values upon which a community builds its foundation. It then expects every individual to follow it. The fear of being left out and alienated ensures one keeps obeying the norms without questioning so much so that they don't dare to ask themselves why they do what they do. They don't discover their passions because they are taught to live life a certain way, express their happiness and joy a certain way and dress and interact with each other a certain way. This compromises the diversity of culture.

Just imagine a society whose foundation is laid on materialism – what kind of values and ideals would it be encouraging?

Social gatherings promote such materialism and have made material possessions as a standard for gaining respect and value. People associate themselves with people of higher stature in order to raise their own status and talk about expensive foreign trips, the car they own, the property they bought and so forth. People get impressed and influenced by these conversations and are pressurised to spend from their pockets; if not, they buy branded bags and shoes on credit in order to fit in. Those who cannot afford this are left out and not valued. The responsibility of breaking such ideals and values lies on the shoulders of the people who can afford luxurious brands but do not set it as a standard for the people who are socially pressurised to keep up with this criteria in order to be respected, when they can hardly make ends meet.

People socialise in order to feel good about themselves, but they are burdened with too much social noise. Social meetups do not add value to their lives but instead are a continuous source of negative energy, comparisons and competition. As a result, in this rat race somewhere along the way, they lose themselves completely. Invitations are 'traded', that is, they should be reciprocated. So if you happen to be invited by someone, you are pressurised to invite them the next time or else you will be talked about in the most nefarious ways. Hence, you land up in a loop of meaningless social gatherings from which it is difficult to get out.

Education itself has become a form of social competence, and the purpose of gaining knowledge has blended into the background. Competition is favoured over personal excellence, leading to many compromises that have to be made. Someone's win is another person's loss, which fosters jealousy amongst each other. The community does not thrive because people don't work together – but against each other. Even work environments pressurise employees through harmless leg-pulling, which lowers creativity and passion among individuals.

There are constant social comparisons and competitions – to throw the best party, to get higher scores than your cousin, to give an expensive gift because the price tag will calculate your worth and so forth.

But, not everyone is strong enough to go against the flow. Some find it difficult to go the opposite way and find it easier to follow the crowd.

Most people conform easily because of the fear of being ridiculed or being thought of as peculiar, or sometimes they have low self-esteem, which does not help realise the better choice. They also follow the crowd because of FOMO (Fear of Missing Out). They want to fit in and seek a sense of belonging.

From the first breath till the last, people live life behind the bars of societal expectations and silently comply with the norms of the society. Dying itself is not easy, because death calls for another set of traditions that are more a burden than a means to show support and comfort to the bereaved family. Life has become entangled in so many irrationalities. Is there anyone who is going to challenge these norms and go against the flow?

The Need for a Divine Code of Ethics
Let me ask a question: Do you possess this mindset of 'submission' as a natural tendency?

Humans have a natural tendency to follow rules and guidelines, and hence they submit to the social limits and rules so naturally. There must be some purpose for it to be present as a part of your natural disposition. If there is no optimum pressure, there will be no achievements and performance. How will you drive the motivation to study for your examinations if you don't have the optimum anxiety needed for you to put in the time and effort?

Societies that lose the values and guidelines completely go astray, where every individual has his or her own set of self-serving values and ideals. It is therefore difficult to coexist in a world where one person's wrong is someone else's right. It is necessary to set up rules or else it becomes impossible to manage a large number of people, each with their own perception of the world and principles of living life.

Who is going to decide where and when you need to obey the norm and when to carve your own set of values and choices? This calls for a standardised code of ethics and principles for every human being to follow for a peaceful coexistence and to be penalised if he or she does not follow the code of conduct. But can this legal conduct be defined by fellow human beings? How neutral would they be? Would they be socially constructed and self-serving values? As long as these social values serve the cause of humanity, they are beneficial. The problem arises when this natural instinct falls in the hands of societies for their own agendas and people become slaves to the whims and desires of others ruling over them. A time comes when they get so entangled that they feel suffocated from these social boundaries and expectations. And if they do not submit, they will be side lined, ignored or ridiculed.

This calls for a divine code upon which the foundation of human ethics is laid, which can become the benchmark to measure any form of deviation. In this way, you are freed from the pressure of obeying people's rules and expectations and your personality becomes a beautiful reflection of your inner self, guided and shaped by divine laws with a unique personal brand. You achieve a balance between submission to rules while at the same time maintaining your individuality by not going with the flow.

ہے ایک سجدہ جسے تو گراں سمجھتا ہے
ہزار سجدے سے دیتا ہے آدمی کو نجات

Prostration 'fore God you presume as irksome, tedious, burden great;
But mind, this homage sets you free from bonds of men, of might who prate!
– Allama Muhammad Iqbal

Summary

Here are some basic steps that you should keep in mind if you want to break free from societal dogmas.

- Silence the social noise around you. Be yourself and don't internalise criticisms.
- Do not become a people pleaser. In the long run, it will suck out all your energy, and you will find yourself caught in a stifling environment that puts your survival at risk. Pleasing your Lord over others should become your criterion; the rest will adjust accordingly.
- Pressure is needed for you to perform as a student to acquire education, as a worker to earn your livelihood, as a parent to raise responsible human beings, as an athlete to deliver your best, as a doctor to save lives. It is you who is going to set the priority of which pressure to take and which to let go. Pick the societal and

- cultural values that serve you and help you grow, and leave the ones that limit you.
- Divine framework frees you from human slavery; hence you live your life on your terms guided by the Divine Light and not manipulated by others.

In the following chapter, we will discuss the kind of people that are highly susceptible to social pressures and how to successfully strike a balance for leading a life of peace and fulfilment.

Chapter Three

Leaky Boundaries

Have you ever experienced in your relationships that no matter how much effort you put in, people always have a complaining attitude towards you? No matter how much you care, people always pick up that one instance when you neglected them. No matter how hard you try to please others, you are never good enough. If this resonates with you, this chapter is going to tell you where you go wrong and what needs to be changed within you so that people will always appreciate your efforts. You will also learn techniques that will ensure you don't get exhausted and burnt out by putting others before your own needs, thus maintaining balanced relationships.

Consider this very common example, which I call 'the middle child syndrome', wherein the first child of the family becomes the centre of attention and the last child is like a cuddly toy for the whole family to play with. The parents are excited at every milestone of their firstborn because they too are experiencing the journey of parenthood for the first time. Enthusiasm is soaring, and if there is another child in the family, she too joins the celebrations. Any challenges and emotional highs and lows are taken care of; no stone is left unturned in making the firstborn child a shining star.

The younger child now believes that her parents' encouragement and interest are a norm and would continue when it is her turn. She anticipates the same treatment, but much to her disappointment, she does not find her cheers reciprocated in the same way. She can easily feel the difference through her parents' lack of energy and disinterest. At this tender age, the child is unable to understand that her parents were actually living their dreams and passions through their first child and that every stage in his or her life was the first one they experienced as a parent. Hence, the interest remained until the outcome and so did the curiosity of what the next stage would hold for them as a parent – a natural human tendency on their part!

The younger child starts to feel left out and is overcome by negative thoughts telling her that she is not good enough to make her parents proud and interested in her wins. This self-criticism does not only lower her self-worth but also makes her an avid seeker of validation and praise – the share that she did not get in her childhood. She tries different ways and means to first please her parents and, later in life, every other person so that she can get her deserved share of attention, recognition and worth. She starts compromising on her boundaries and eventually may become a doormat for the world to misuse. People having similar experiences in life display leaky boundaries. They try to become the best towards people in search of appreciation and validation compromising over their self-worth.

On the flip side, people tend to create very rigid boundaries with zero tolerance ensuring that others do not break their rules. They often use the method of conditioning to set certain standards that they do not want others to challenge or override. There is an old wives' tale in South Asian culture where the newlywed groom is recommended to kill the cat the very night of his nuptial. This means that he should clearly communicate the dos and don'ts in a very non-negotiable manner. In order to ensure he always has an upper hand over his wife, he should show her the non-flexible, stern side of his personality and scare her so that she does not dare to step over the set boundary. This is what was believed to 'live like a lion' or to 'kill the cat on the very first night'. Now the question here is about the boundaries that you have set for your spouse – how sure are you that they are absolutely the right set of rules and will positively impact the well-being of your relationship? In fact, this approach can leave lifelong scars on your marital bond and cripple your beautiful relationship with your spouse.

Conditioning and reinforcement are good techniques when used wisely – just like a weapon, which when handed to a fool can result in a crime, but if used for self-defence can indeed be useful. Similarly, you can reinforce rules and set good standards through conditioning. For example, the same principle of killing the cat can be put to excellent use to train a child to have a proper bedtime routine by being consistent in your expectations and having zero tolerance to late shows at breakfast from the very first day of the rule. By not allowing flexibility or relaxation in the rule, you can ensure your child takes the routine seriously.

A boundary is an imaginary wall between you and the other person. It is a kind of self-defence tool that protects you from any harm that can be caused due to unwarranted expectations or projections of others onto you.

Boundaries can be of different kinds: personal boundaries, workplace boundaries, physical and emotional boundaries, financial boundaries and so forth.

The Drama Triangle
The Rescuer
People who don't secure themselves by having healthy boundaries are the unhappiest and loneliest people. While they are always there to provide all kinds of help and support to others, in the times that they need others, there's no one to help them. To add to their disappointment, others hold grudges of the times such people did not help them.

Rescuers have leaky boundaries. They put themselves and their needs last. They hold this strange and dangerous belief that they don't have the right to self-care and owe their life to others. Thus, they deprive themselves of basic needs like not getting enough sleep, sacrificing their interests over others or spending money to meet the needs of others.

This kind of sacrifice is often confused with the sacrifice that we do for pleasing our Lord. You may nicely wrap things under a religious pretext and you may think that your behaviour is an appreciated one from a religious angle. However, there's a fine line between spiritual sacrifice and leaky boundaries. The former is a type of sacrifice to please God, while the latter is a sacrifice to please people so as to be in their good books. Spiritual sacrifice makes you strong by encouraging you to practise self-control, while leaky boundaries turn you into a football – you are kicked around by the desires and wishes of others, leaving you physically and emotionally bruised. Often you may compromise your physical health by going out of your way to help others and ignoring your health that might need some serious attention.

Sometimes you hold certain beliefs, even in the spiritual realm, which if are not within context could be mishandled.

For example, there was a man who had this very absolute and unbalanced belief that if he will help others, Allah will help him and his family in times of need. There is no harm in having this belief so long as it does not make you lose balance. In fact, it will benefit you as you are actually supported by Allah. But when the balance is lost and things are understood out of the context, you could actually deplete yourself and your family physically, financially and most importantly emotionally.

When your family becomes second to all the others that you are helping under the belief that this would relieve your family, you are neglecting your family to the point they are deprived of their basic rights because you are busy helping – and oftentimes being used by – others to fulfil their needs.

When you have the belief that you are born a superhero that is there to help others, you forget that your foremost responsibility is your own family. They look forward to your resources, including your time, which you may be spending generously in helping others, thereby leaving your own family orphaned and at the mercy of circumstances. This results in emptiness and frustration in your relationships with your loved ones because of unfulfilled needs and responsibilities for they know very well that no matter what, you will prioritise others over them.

The man in the above example never realised that his belief was very relative and subjective. The results he saw were from a selective vision; he was unaware of the heavy cost he was paying to maintain this belief and enjoys its selective fruits.

Belief is a very tricky thing. It is an algorithm that fits in your brain and starts producing outcomes that you desire. No matter what you believe, it finds a way for you. This is why people, despite having contradicting beliefs, find their wishes being fulfilled. Then why is it even important to evaluate your beliefs? Keep on believing whatever you are conditioned to and the algorithm will give the results. Just like this man who sacrificed himself and his family by putting them second, giving himself wholeheartedly to the belief he held, one has to also see the compromises and sacrifices to be made in order to get his or her win. What losses did he and his family bear in order to get the much-sought win and was it was worth the deal? What belief could have been a better and balanced alternative in order to achieve the same outcome?

What beliefs can give you the most wins and minimal loss in this world and also in the hereafter is the question you need to keep asking yourself in order to optimise your life.

A person with unhealthy boundaries has serious communication issues because he finds it difficult to say no. Lacking clear communication skills, he often beats about the bush which creates miscommunication and confusion in relationships.

This disease to please others compels him to make unrealistic commitments; for example, he may accept multiple invites at similar times, overcommit and underdeliver at work and push himself to do things which he is humanly incapable of. This could lead him to miscalculate time and other resources. People often recognise this as a weakness and try to play around it by taking advantage of his kind nature. They ask him for favours when they know he will always answer in the positive. In order to satisfy his shattered self-esteem, he feels pride in the fact that people approach him when they are in need, but he overlooks the fact that they are misusing him for their advantage, avoiding doing the hard work that they should do themselves. Such people with unhealthy boundaries are usually a misfit in managerial job roles because they do not know how to delegate tasks to team members and how to extract work from them. Instead, the team will rule over the manager and exploit his empathy. As a result, his team does not work efficiently and is not productive in meeting targets.

Self-Talk
'I must help you.'
'Only I can fix this.'
'If I don't help, it will be so selfish of me.'
'If someone asks for help, I should help him.'

As a rescuer, you will have these feelings: anxiety, pity, excitement, pride.

In our society, we often see that people are purposely trained to let go off their needs and become a people pleaser. Often, religion is exploited and manipulated in order to raise such doormats that are trained to serve society by putting others' needs over their own. Most often, when seeking a girl for marriage, people prefer a girl who is trained to compromise from early childhood over a strong-willed female who knows herself and prioritises her self-care over people's expectations and demands. People often label such women as self-centred and selfish, because they are not willing to be manipulated and blackmailed.

The reason behind the unfulfilled relationships of a rescuer type often goes back into his or her childhood and upbringing during the tender years – for example, what values he holds supreme and what beliefs he has been raised with. Sometimes, children are raised in environments with poor financial resources, or parents may place the child into the role of a caretaker of the family's emotional and financial needs. Mostly children who are compassionate, caring and have a lot of empathy towards others naturally adopt this role, or they may have an elder in the family from whom they learn this behaviour.

The Victim
This group of people are those who from childhood have not been given the confidence to make their own decisions. They have been ridiculed for their choices and bullied all their life. Hence, they have low self-esteem. In challenging situations, they are overwhelmed by their own vulnerability and do not take responsibility for their own situation. They always look for a shoulder to which they can shift the responsibility, and if anything goes wrong, they place the blame on others.

The victim, because of his over-reliance on others, has high expectations from others. He drains the energy of people helping him. No matter how hard others try to empower him, he is not willing to fly on his own.

You cannot help someone who does not want to help himself.

Self-Talk
'Poor me, this always happens to me.'
'I can never do this on my own.'
'If someone does not help me, I will lose.'
'I don't know what to do.'
'Nobody cares for me. I am lonely.'
'My life is so difficult.'

You will have the following feelings: distress, panic, helplessness, resentment of others, irritation, smallness and fragility.

The Persecutor
This group of people find themselves in a state where they have no energy left to serve others, such that they become self-centred and lose empathy altogether. Here's a gentle soul who has hardened over time due to over-giving beyond capacity and doing too many compromises and sacrifices in the past. Such people tend to reach another extreme of 'I-don't-care' attitude, carrying baggage of resentment, stress and depression for a long time resulting in the loss of physical health.

This realisation mostly dawns when you have spent almost your entire life pleasing people and despite having compromised valuable portions of your life, people still do not recognise your service. With the decline in both your energy and resources, you harden up and reach a stage where you are left with no compassion and empathy for others, leading you to engage in destructive relationships.

Self-Talk
'I know what we need to do.'
'I know what you need to do.'
'You don't know what you are talking about.'
'We both know that I'm right.'
'Oh!' (in a disappointed tone)
'Shame!
'Why are you crying again?'
'No one agrees with you.'

In this state, you will feel physically tense, hot and bothered. You will feel resentful and cross.

You will realise that you are moving across this triangle from time to time, switching between these three roles. Your movement on this triangle can either be rapid or can be played out over weeks, months or years.

Escaping the Drama Triangle and Building Healthy Boundaries

In order to have a balanced relationship, you need to have healthy boundaries. Often people think that boundaries create distance in relationships; however, this is not the case. In fact, they define the relationship on mutual terms and help in improving and sustaining the relationship.

If you have a leaky boundary, chances are that you have made others comfortable in putting you second. Why then does everyone treat you in a similar manner, and why don't they treat each other in the same way? This clearly proves that it is you who has allowed others to cross the limit and treat you in this manner.

The Empowerment Triangle

The reason I have gone over the pains of having an undefined relationship is to make you realise that it is never too late to set healthy boundaries. You may think that you cannot change, and people will not accept the new you. Yes, initially it may be difficult, and your relationships could go through a rough ride because you have become a changed person. Accepting change is always difficult. Especially when it does not favour other people, it could result in shock for them as they did not expect this to happen. Most of their complaining is because they are no longer able to control and manipulate you as per their wishes and desires. However, if you stay firm, their bitterness fades away, often resulting in their own self-realisation, giving them an opportunity to dive deeper into themselves and unveiling the emotional complexities of their lives. The practice of maintaining healthy boundaries of your newly discovered self while building new relationships will make you persistent in your endeavours.

From Rescuer to Coach

People with leaky boundaries are excellent problem-solvers and hence people are easily attracted to them. Helping people in trouble and freeing them from their distress is an act of worship as long as you are not foregoing the rights and responsibilities of your Lord, yourself and those who are made dependent on you.

There's a litmus test for you to check your motivation behind helping others – whether you're giving them a free ride home, helping people in your workplace or cooking a meal for your neighbour. Look at the cost you have to pay for going that extra mile. Make sure that it is not at the cost of neglecting the rights of God upon you, by missing your obligatory prayers, or neglecting the rights of yourself upon you, by continuously compromising your sleep or physical and emotional health. You also need to check whether you are depriving the rights of those dependent on you, who look forward to your support whether in the form of time, energy or money. Are you fulfilling your obligations before you go and become a saviour of those outside? You may be neglecting your near ones, and they too might be seeking a saviour because of your inattention.

For you to draw a line and not exhaust yourself, you need to understand that you are a human being. You have limited time, limited energy, limited provisions and other resources. You are not the ultimate Benevolent who has limitless power and capacity to fulfil the need of others. For example, it is Allah's limitless power that enables you to become a source of help and service to others. Your incapacity and limited nature make you realise that you cannot rescue the world no matter how hard you try, if Allah does not will. You are neither omnipresent nor can you provide for everyone or alter the destiny of the less fortunate. The moment you have the realisation of your incapacity, you prioritise things and are able to let go of the self-pressure that you often put on yourself. You become easy on yourself and will not feel guilty of self-care when you give yourself time to recover/recharge before you proceed to serve others.

We often compare the level of generosity and service to others that is expected from us to the ways of the earlier generations. Consider these two scenarios: A traveller knocks on your door and asks for shelter. You provide him with the basic needs and food and take good care of him while he is in your company. This was the usual compassionate way of how people used to help each other in the past.

Now take the second scenario. A person calls you when it is your time to spend with your family. You feel the urge to leave your family waiting so that you can serve his request, because according to you serving humanity equals serving the Lord. You are helping him at the expense of your family needs. Can his request wait? Yes, it can for an appropriate time when you are free to take his call.

You are from a different generation, where distances have shrunk, time itself beats the clock and the magnitude of unwelcome intrusions is uncountable. Hence comparing values of earlier generations in a technologically paced world and finding yourself replying to welcome or unwelcome intrusions can burden you to an extent that people in the past did not experience. Neither is the WhatsApp caller in a situation similar to that of the destitute traveller.

However, the divine laws are timeless, and the Quran teaches us how to have healthy boundaries. At the start of Chapter 49, 'The Chamber' (Al-Hujurat), Allah commands the believers to have proper etiquettes while addressing the Prophet and to not raise their voices to call him out of his chamber during his resting time. So that the Prophet could put his tired body – which endlessly toiled for his Lord – to rest, Allah made sure that people do not disturb him when they had queries to be answered or needs to be taken care of.

- Self-care is not only looking after your health and well-being, your own concerns and interests. It is also about 'receiving' help, love and support when you need it from others. The transition from a giving to a receiving position is necessary for you to reach a balance in relationships where there is an equal share of give and take from both sides and none of you is depleted of your energy and resources in going overboard to maintain a relationship single-handedly.
- Build a boundary around technology too. Take time off from the digital world by installing applications that limit your time on the Internet.

- Honour yourself, accept your limitations, have pure intentions, do what you can to help others without compromising your priorities. When it is beyond your capacity, leave it to Allah and pray for their betterment.
- Become a role model for your children. Make sure they don't learn the wrong values from you and carry them forward to the next generation.

From Victim to Creator

Alternatively, you should make sure that you are not leaning hard on someone so much that you become totally dependent on his support. Initially, you may enjoy it because offloading your worries and tensions onto someone else will make you feel lighter, but shifting your burdens onto someone else does not go a long way.

No matter how selfless that person is, if he is expected to carry your burden for a long time, it will create a gap and perhaps bitterness between you two. He will have to set a strong boundary in order to push you away. You are no longer a child who looks for nurture and comfort from his mother whenever he needs support. You have to row your boat yourself; people can help you sometimes but not always. You need to learn problem-solving skills and empower yourself through continued growth and learning. Personal growth will boost your self-esteem and will stop you from unnecessary reliance on others.

From Persecutor to Challenger

- A challenger is assertive. He learns from the past and does not take it with him like baggage. He is forward-looking and despite all the past hurt, he frees his mental space by forgiving whatever happened in the past.

- He learns constructive ways of meeting his needs without punishing others.
- He not only challenges himself to grow but also calls forth growth in others.

Once you let go of your past self, you will find that your emotional health will improve. You won't be carrying the baggage of resentment or unfulfilled expectations – and also no longer a bruised you.

You will get clarity in your relationships where you and others stand. The expectations in your relationships will be well managed and will ensure that you don't give beyond your capacity. You will learn a constructive way to meet your needs without punishing others. Soon you will understand the importance of self-care.

You will realise that you cannot make everyone happy. People will start valuing you despite you not giving 100% in the relationship and stop taking you for granted. Your efforts are valued and are not thankless. Even if you don't seek appreciation, the intention is important! Your effort should be to please Allah and not the people. You should not become the slaves of other people's desires and wishes.

This shift in perception will free you from human slavery. Always remember that no one is going to help or support you in creating healthy boundaries for yourself. You have to take a step forward towards your personal growth. Building healthy boundaries and overcoming social pressures will give you the freedom to accept yourself, which we will discuss in the next chapter. It will allow you to take a journey within yourself, eliminating your personal negative beliefs, limiting blocks and external pressures imposed on by your surroundings.

This will allow you to reach a beautiful balance where you will know how to utilise your limited provisions wisely and efficiently in order to feel a sense of fulfilment. You will be at peace with yourself and your surroundings, without letting go of your gentle and compassionate side.

Summary

- People with leaky boundaries give beyond their capacity hence compromise over their self-care.
- People with rigid boundaries build strong walls around them.
- You cannot make everyone happy.
- Healthy boundaries empower you to have balanced relationships.
- Having healthy boundaries ensures that your expectations are well managed.

Chapter Four

I Love Being Naked

Break Free
What is the first and foremost thing that impedes you from letting go of social pressures or building healthy boundaries? It is your fears and insecurities that cage you. Feel the freedom; break free.

I like facing my fears instead of being a turtle that hides in its shell. Yes, I love being naked. I hate wearing layers over my soul to impress others. There is nothing as pleasurable as acceptance!

Fear of Abandonment
Many people in society are afraid of going against the wishes of their loved ones and losing associations. This makes them people-pleasers that cannot build relationships on mutually serving terms. They are easily blackmailed at the hands of their loved ones. A typical male of a South Asian society is manipulated by his mother in the name of religion. He is bombarded with self-serving religious doctrines the moment his mother thinks that she is losing control over him. Emotional blackmailing is another powerful tool wherein the parent may dramatise his or her health condition so the child submits to the parent's demands and wishes.

Consider this typical situation in a South Asian household. The girl does not have the luxury to let go of social pressures and carve a life of her own. Let's discuss what form of insecurities she has and what are its roots. I should warn you before proceeding, because what you read is going to unveil some hard and bitter realities of our society and will require courage and acceptance on your part.

A typical girl of South Asian background has the pressure to look good in ways that align with the set standards. This means that despite having a brown skin tone, she will not be allowed to embrace her youthful skin and will be forced to use artificial products to give her a fairer look because fairness is the standard of beauty in society. What fear holds her back in accepting her skin tone? Yes, she will be rejected many times when she serves tea to a dozen families who are on the hunt for pretty young girls (whatever the definition of 'pretty' might be). Chances are that despite her educational achievements and intellect, she may not get a suitable proposal and be forced to spend the rest of her life single and dejected.

The girls who meet the criteria have the opportunity to tie the knot. But are these married women allowed to live a life of their own will? What are the pressures that daughters-in-law face, and what are the fears that stop them from building safe boundaries? Why do daughters-in-law proffer special, entitled treatment to their in-laws, giving in to their every want, while overlooking their own needs? Why are sons-in-law only given royal treatment, while the opposite is not true? Why a married woman will not refuse dinner invites from in-laws at any cost even if that means compromising her primary needs or cancelling her prior commitments? She will spend most of her time and energy looking after the household chores in a joint family despite having children who need more attention and care. Why will she prefer taking care of her mother-in-law over her own mother in case both are sick at the same time? Is it really for the sake of Allah and for pleasing her husband? Why does the key to her husband's pleasure lie in her being a doormat to his family? She might claim that she does it out of love for him, but what is the underlying fear that she is unable to overcome? Yes, the fear of abandonment, the fear of divorce, the fear of her husband's second marriage! Divorcees have no place of respect in our society; they are proclaimed guilty without even being trialled, while co-wives are looked down upon with pity. Even if they do not feel so, society will make sure they feel insufficient. What is the big deal in being a divorcee? Life certainly does not come to an end, and the feminist cries are valid – that you don't need a man to survive! Who will marry a divorcee in this society, where there is already a long queue of not so pretty virgins waiting? But do you think this is a sustainable model of existence without the need to remarry, irrespective of gender?

The plight of widows is nothing different, and they too are abandoned. If a divorcee or a widow is blessed with a living father, she is still taken care of, but if she has to live with her brother she is suppressed and dejected as if she is a burden or an unwanted piece of furniture. If she decides to live all by herself, the society does not spare her from the devouring eyes of men looking for a one-night stand.

Temporarily, self-sustenance looks quite attractive, but in case she has children to look after, single-parent families know the psychological pain they go through to survive in this world. I deliberately do not mention the financial challenges they may face, because today's women are able enough to earn a livelihood for their children; however, the cost they have to pay is a large sum that many will never understand. The cost of giving up her own desires – be it sexual or emotional – is a very large sum to pay. She has to sacrifice a lot by compromising her primary needs in order to look after the children who are dependent on her. Later in life, her expectations and demands from her children become very high because of the trauma and stress that she has borne throughout her life. The children, no matter how much they try, are not able to reciprocate these sacrifices. They fail to meet the unrealistic expectations, and she becomes a heavy baggage for them to carry.

So, what should a woman do if she cannot accept the injustice and oppression that she has to face? The other choice that she is left with is to compromise and live a life of fear as an oppressed woman, without raising her voice against the injustice. By giving in too much against her will, she loses out on her health. Although she gains some control over her life with every passing year as her children grow older, but by the time she reaches her 50s, her physical and psychological health does not allow her to live the life she had dreamt of.

The question is, how can we give women a voice against oppression so that they don't compromise their values and can bargain for a life that they deserve? So that they can overcome the fear of abandonment and take a strong, powerful stand without having to face the consequences. Can we promise them freedom from the compromised and oppressed life that they have been living and are we willing to provide them social security? Or will taking a stand demand future compromises and oppression but in a different way? Keeping in mind that it could be you, your sister or daughter, are you willing to support and embrace them with open arms? Are we willing to accept divorcees and widows as the wives of our sons or as our co-wives or of our daughters? Indeed, these are very hard questions to answer.

The purpose of writing this is to let women know their worth. Let them live a life driven by their own passions without compromising their natural desires and without living a life of fear – the fear of being a divorcee, the fear of being a co-wife!

Fear of Failure
What stops you from pursuing your passions?

There are two kinds of people who do not have the fear of failure. First are the ones who have enough support and stability to take risks, while the second are those who have nothing to risk and nothing to lose. Both these kinds can be adventurous in trying out new things and will not hesitate in pursuing their passions. The rest of the lot plays safe and avoids taking risks; they live a routine life, work nine to five to secure their job, have an income stable enough to run their family and enjoy some recreational activities.

What is the common factor between the two kinds of people that I just mentioned? It is an abundance of provisions and security, or nothing at all. If you do chase your dream, you stand to lose all your provisions. The fear of losing your provisions sounds really scary. You tend to think of all the negative things that might happen if you jump in. Adding to the negative self-talk, there will be people who will give you examples of a certain person and how he failed because he left his job and followed a business venture. It is time to prove such people wrong. What if you focus on all the positive things that could come your way if you pursue your passions? Thus, your mind will be wired to possibilities and opportunities instead of being constantly driven by what might go wrong.

> *'Tell your heart that the fear of suffering is worse than the suffering itself. And that no heart has ever suffered when it goes in search of its dreams, because every second of the search is a second's encounter with God and with eternity.'*
> – Paulo Coelho, The Alchemist

Also, how about having this presupposition that your provision is pre-defined, calculated and measured. You will only get your pre-destined share, nothing more and nothing less. With this belief strongly embedded in your brain – provided you are not stuck in logics and arguments looking for empirical evidence to support it – you will leave no stone unturned in materialising your dream.

You will step out of your comfort zone, taking bold steps with calculated risks, embracing failures and setbacks as part of the process. These temporary setbacks and obstacles will not demoralise you. You will keep going, treating the failures as feedback that teaches you how to navigate better in the future.

> *'Life is all about successes and failures unless you are lazing around in your comfort zone.'*

Have you ever participated in an obstacle race? Every obstacle in the way teaches you a better skill on how to move across the future challenges more efficiently.

There is a difference between loss and failure. We often think they are the same. Your failure <u>can</u> lead to a loss if you give up, but it can turn into success if you keep going. You lose when you give up.

> *'There are no shortcuts in life. To unlock the door of your destiny, you have to try every other door on your way only to be struck down by disappointment and dismay, but to rise again climbing over all obstacles before you finally unlock your fate. The key to that door is Keep Going!'*

I won't say don't be afraid of failures; that's still a defensive approach. Instead, say, **'I love to fail because in failure I learn the best lessons of my life.'** This obviously does not mean that you purposely make mistakes in order to fail. I believe when you get addicted to the pearls of wisdom that come along with it, you will actually crave it. Successes and failures come in cycles. I prefer cherishing both of them equally and enjoying them both as life's natural order. The ultimate success is a combination of this pattern.

Rather than getting demoralised by your setbacks, power through them. They should become the reason for your perseverance. Keep on challenging yourself, and in this process, you will realise how much you have grown out of your comfortable shell.

Accepting your Limitation

> *'In this result-oriented world, don't be too hard on yourself. It is always a good idea to relax, take a pause and PRAY.'*

We often hear this notion that everything is possible. Well, it does motivate you to push yourself further while at the same time it drains your energy because you keep unrealistic expectations. Eventually, reality will hit you hard because there will be times that no matter how much you try, things do not work out.

It is at this place when you should, after giving your 100%, place your faith in the Almighty and leave things to fate. You will learn that the only Doer and Absolute Being is just One, and, for Him, nothing is impossible. This will give you the hope and power to get up again and try another way instead of losing hope, feeling depressed and eventually becoming suicidal.

> *'Nothing is Impossible for Him.'*

Remember, persistence does not mean insistence and stubbornness. Maintain a commitment to the truth and not to consistent actions for an outcome that is away from the truth.

It is always wise to accept the natural order of the universe and go with the natural flow of life.

'It is not allowable for the sun to reach the moon, nor does the night overtake the day, but each, in an orbit, is swimming.'
– (Quran – 36:40)

I remember the days when my children had started school and I wanted to go back to work. I had been depleted of energy and was frustrated because of the monotony in my life. I started searching for jobs. Being a high achiever, I had been readily recruited in the early days of my career, but given the long gap now, I was unsure this time. However, I was very desperate to work. I got an interview call from a company, and I rejoiced that my resume still had the power to catch attention. Filled with self-belief, I entered the interview room. The interview went really well and they offered me a very good package. I was assured that I will get the appointment letter very soon.

Much to my dismay, two weeks passed, and I never heard from them. After waiting for a long time, I followed up with them only to know that they had a sudden change of plans, and the vacancy I had interviewed for was no longer available. Being an HSP (Highly Sensitive Person), I feel things on a much deeper level. I remember those weeks of anticipation. With each passing day, the clouds got darker and I was drawn into depression. No amount of self-belief was sufficient because Allah had different plans for me. Had I known how beautiful my journey would turn out to be, I wouldn't have felt so low. But these low moments gave me the power to rediscover my truest passions. My love for psychology took me on a journey of self-discovery. Had I got that job I would have never discovered the work that I love the most – my love of bringing ease into other people's lives by using my talent and potential as a Life Coach. I discovered how much I enjoy playing with words. From being a blogger to an author, each and every moment – whether in my favour or against me – became a moment of patience and gratitude.

This memory of frustration and depression gives me power in those times when I feel stuck, when nothing seems to be working out. It gives me hope that there is light at the end of the tunnel. If Allah wills, it is meant to be. If He does not, no amount of hard work or self-belief can change His plans. I surrender my limited self to the Limitless Being!

Accepting Your Outer Self

Certain self-limiting beliefs – such as your house should be in order all the time, you should be smiling all the time, you should be looking good all the time, you should be perfect – can drain you unnecessarily.
The third step is to start accepting yourself the way you have been created, inside and out.

When you start accepting yourself, you accept your body. Whether you are tall or short, dark or fair, young or old, you don't fake yourself. If you don't accept the way you were created, you will live in a state of denial.

When you are in denial, it is often very difficult to accept all parts of yourself. Remember your whole is divided into many parts, some good and some not so good. Accepting each and every part of yourself as your own will give you the freedom to open and embrace the imperfect you.

Some parts – both inner and outer – can never be changed. These define your individuality. There was a boy who was very good looking, smart and intelligent. He was a high-performance learner at school and had very good social relationships with his peers. However, his mother noticed something strange about him. She observed that he would never wear sandals or any footwear that would expose his feet in public. Even if he had to take off his footwear at places like a mosque, he would ensure he had his socks on. Out of curiosity, his mother asked him for the reason behind this. At first, he was reluctant to answer, but then he suddenly burst into tears. He told his mother that he had very ugly feet and he did not want to expose them in front of others. He had been bullied by one of his friends and from that day he stopped showing his feet to anyone. His mother changed his perception of how he sees his feet as dictated by his peer and made him realise how Allah has created him from His will and that these were the feet selected by the One who loves him the most: *'who created you, proportioned you, and balanced you? In whatever form He willed has He assembled you'* (Quran 82:7,8).

Her mother taught him a very important lesson: to accept himself the way he has been created and to fully embrace his individuality without letting any outside pressure compel him to alter it.

For example, if you are an introvert, forcing yourself to fit into a loud social crowd is not who you are. Don't force yourself. Accept that you draw your energy from solitude and reflection. Take your time and gain energy before you are back in the social world. Don't hesitate to excuse yourself from your friends and family. They will understand you if you truly understand and accept yourself.

Similarly, if you are short, you cannot grow taller by stretching your body a few more inches. It is your genetic structure. Embrace it without putting on heels to look what you are not. There is no harm wearing heels if you love to, but a misleading thought like this could damage your self-esteem.

Perfection Paralysis

There are certain parts of you that can be upgraded over time by putting some efforts. The stubborn mindset of accepting yourself the way you are –

'I am the way I am' – will lead to stagnancy. Through learning and experience, you can work on your flaws. But before you can work on them, you have to accept them. It is only then you will make an effort to improve and change. Change is the secret sauce to growth, but many people are not flexible enough to change and hence remain in the same situation, in the same position for years both personally and professionally. Always remember: *If nothing changes, nothing changes!*

For example, seeking perfection in everything is a flaw. If you are compulsive and obsessed with perfection in your work, you will not be happy with yourself, and neither can anyone please you because your level of expectations from yourself and others are too high to be met realistically.

Perfection is a mirage, and like most people, you run after it. You burden yourself, never satisfied with your efforts. As a result, your self-talk is all about self-criticism, devaluing your work and not thinking highly of yourself. This will put a lot of pressure on you. Don't fall in the trap of being perfect. The story that you tell yourself builds your self-esteem. It is very important that the story gives hope and positivity.

You are an imperfect human, so it is useless to be in competition with Him. You won't reach His Perfection. You can strive for excellence and continue putting efforts in moving towards perfection, but at the same time know that you cannot reach there no matter how hard you try. But then it is good to be as close to it as possible. This will liberate you from high expectations of yourself that keep you stuck from moving forward and paralyse you from taking practical steps. You will start taking little steps at a time, each one better than the previous – but not perfect. You will keep learning and improvising as you continue to move forward.

Accept the different states in you. You are a spiritual being with bodily needs. You will have your highs and lows, and it is okay. There will be times when you'll be so high on energy that you will be out there to conquer the world, and there will be days when you won't feel like getting out of bed. Your life will be filled with both laughter and tears. There is no need to feel bad about yourself, as this is the natural order of the universe and, as a part of it, you follow suit. There are signs in alterations of the night and day. In fact, constancy leads to boredom. Just imagine if there was just one season throughout the year! The beauty of spring would lose its worth. Absence increases fondness. How will you admire the good if you don't experience the bad?

Many people are obsessed with looking young. They do not accept the natural order of the universe. They want to stop time. No wonder there is a huge market for Botox and antiwrinkle products. People get depressed as soon as their physical health starts declining, because they expected that they will stay the same throughout life. Since this was more of a fantasy, when reality hits, it hits very hard. Embrace every stage of your life. Do not shy away in telling your age; flaunt your grey hair! Your skin will not be the same as before, but your blemishes will shine proudly. With every passing decade, your skin may sag more, your face will wrinkle more and more – but every fold will have a story to tell. A story of passion, a story of strength, a story of courage and when you reach your final resting place, you will be feeling proud of the legacy that you would have left behind before you transition into immortality.

Go with the natural flow of life. Enjoy every moment by accepting it the way it is, rather than wishing the way it should. Let go of the desire to bring back time. Breathe!

People who are usually obsessed with perfection have a fear of failure and vice versa. Initially you will find it difficult to overcome this compulsion.

If you remind yourself that Absolute is just the One who is All Seeing All Present, All Sufficient, while you are a creation who needs sleep and food for survival. You live in a relative world where every next effort will be better than the last one.

People get obsessed with perfect living, perfect parenting, perfect marriage, perfect job and perfect grades so much so that they expect 10/10 from their children, and, if they do not perform, parents do not accept them. See how the lack of acceptance is ingrained in childhood and how badly it impacts our self-esteem. Never ask your child, *'Why did you score low?'* Instead ask him, 'What did you learn?' and tell him, *'There is always a next time.'*

In this need to be the perfect parent and to have a good outer image, parents become conscious when young children throw a tantrum in public. It is okay, don't be embarrassed or give in to their demands just to maintain that perfect image because people are watching. Just politely apologise for the situation by saying your child is having a bad day.

As a parent, you cannot be present everywhere at the same time to observe and correct everything that needs to be taken care of. Hence you will have many blind spots while raising your children, and that is perfectly okay. There is nothing such as perfect parenting. Relax and be easy on yourself.

> *'You have a fear of failure because you put yourself on a very high pedestal; hence you get stuck by not even trying. Get over it! There exist billions and trillions of creations in this world, and you are a minute dot in comparison. Come on, relax! It is okay to fail and learn from your setbacks. A child knows this secret, and that's how he grows. Learn from him.*

> *Also, you might be a small dot, but you are the best of creations. The best because you have the power to choose. So, what are you choosing: Growth or Dormancy?'*

Be Vulnerable

Once you accept yourself, let others accept you too. Do not shy away from expressing your emotions with your near and dear ones. It is the key to effective communication and stronger relationships. Whether with your parents, spouse, children or friends, accept your flaws; do not hide from or defend them. Accept when you are wrong. Model to your children that it is okay to make mistakes, that we humans can never be flawless. Show them how you are continuously making efforts to improve yourself and become a better version of yourself. It will eliminate the unnecessary noise and distortion in your communication with them. And in return, they too will open up and share their real side with you, and together you can grow and improve.

Once you are strong enough to let your fears go and stop looking for validation from others, you will have come a long way in your journey of rediscovery. Always remember that for you to reach this stage, you will have to pass through a long period of darkness. There will be times where you feel completely lost, and something will be breaking within for the divine light to enter and enlighten your soul. However, these testing times will be the most insightful periods of your life. The masks that you had been wearing for so long will start to dissolve, and the beautiful you will begin to radiate through it. Your newly discovered self will feel empowered, loved and appreciated by you and will become a valuable asset for your surroundings. All those lost connections, betrayals and low points of life will fade away. You will become such a source of positivity for others that the society to whom you always looked for validation will now long for your presence.

Summary

- Fear is **F**alse Evidence **A**ppearing **R**eal. Encounter it and fight it with faith. If you truly believe that there is a Higher Power who will always be your safety net, you will never stop taking that leap of faith whenever it is necessary for your growth.
- Once you let go of your fears, you break free from all negative beliefs.
- Accept yourself the way you have been created. Flow with the natural order of the universe.
- Accept your limitations.
- Accept your flaws because it is only then you will take a step in overcoming them.
- Do not run after perfection; failure is your classroom.

Chapter Five

Tick-Tock Goes the Clock

Imagine you are on an island and you have been handed a pouch full of gold coins to fulfil your needs. You cannot look inside to count the coins, but as long as something is inside, you can survive. On what things are you going to spend these coins? Will you set any priorities, or will you immediately buy the first thing you see? I am sure you will be very cautious spending these coins, mindful of where you are spending and of the return on investment (ROI) if you happen to invest them. Is it worth investing in? You will be doing calculations in your mind so you can utilise this limited resource in the best way possible.

What if you are robbed of some coins? What will be your reaction? Most of you will truly feel a loss, saddened upon losing your treasured asset. However, do you know that you often lose something that can never be earned back no matter how much you try? It is limited and numbered. Not a penny less, not a penny more! By now you may have guessed I'm referring to time – an asset that despite being intangible is worth more than gold or silver, a mansion or a Rolls Royce, or your latest gadget or anything else material that you may assign value to.

'Time is the quantifiable representation of a human life; hence it is the most valued asset a human possesses.'

Purpose – Your Unique Code

It is very tragic how one undervalues the time and spends it so wastefully. Although, the moment you realise its importance, it is then you understand the meaning of your life and reason for your existence. Your existence has a purpose. Every single breath is a journey towards it. The moment it is reached, your time is up. Not a breath more, not a breath less!

Most of you are completely oblivious to your purpose. Always remember, you will not be handed your purpose on a plate for you to go and fulfil it. It requires effort on your part, sometimes years of hard work, reflection and contemplation to discover the true purpose for which you have been created, because nothing in this world is created without a reason. With this awareness, you will consciously seek your true purpose.

> *'Every human has a unique cryptograph embedded with his or her genetic code. It is called PURPOSE. Decipher it to unveil your inner self and make impactful impressions in your life and that of others.'*

Your purpose will be hidden in your strengths and weaknesses alike. You need to accept yourself the way you have been created along with your strengths and shortcomings – as discussed in the previous chapters – only then can you discover your potential. You go through a long journey of fulfilling your human needs before you transcend and reach your ultimate purpose, as stated by Abraham Maslow in his hierarchy of needs. Therefore, it is advisable to fulfil your primary needs as early in your life as possible so that your basic needs do not distract you from reaching the self-actualised state. However, the power of belief is strong enough to even overcome the hurdles of your basic needs, and you may strive to explore your inner self, irrespective of your situation.

Maslow's Hierarchy of Needs

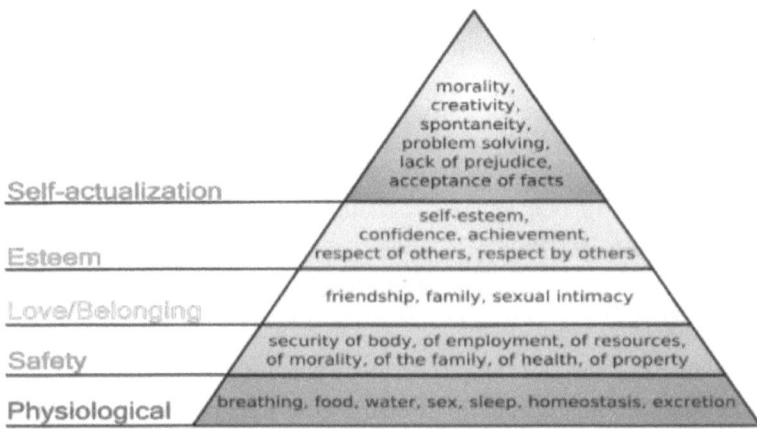

The beliefs that your birth and death are pre-written, that your provisions are already allocated and promised to you until the time of your death, that your marital bond is pre-written and that the provider of respect and recognition is the Almighty reduce the anxieties and fears that accompany their attainment. Hence, at every stage of your life – irrespective of the situation you might be in – it is possible for you to reflect and decode your true purpose, because this is the only thing whose accomplishment has not been promised by Allah. These pre-suppositions give you the courage to dream big and to unleash your true potential. You keep going without having any fear whatsoever. Your continuous struggle leads you to set higher goals in life, living a prosocial life. A life of impact; a life of a legend. This is how an Edhi is born in a nation.

> *'The realisation that your life has a purpose is in itself the journey half done.'*

Once you find direction in your life and with it a roadmap to achieve your targets and realise your dreams, you are very cautious of those gold coins in your pouch. You cannot spend them lavishly and unnecessarily. Neither do you have the power to preserve them, no matter how much you fantasise watching Marvel Studios.

However, despite this awareness, you waste your time in multiple ways without realising that you are actually losing the gold coins without receiving a justified ROI. Sometimes your expenditure becomes more of a liability than an asset. For example, how much time do you spend daily in wasting away your life in stress and depression? A continuous train of thoughts consumes you completely, and you go into never-ending assumptions and possibilities, building scenario after scenario that may arise due to a hypothetical situation – a situation that is just the creation of your mind and the probability of its manifestation is the same as that of putting toothpaste back in the tube.

The Ways in Which You Waste Your Time

When you value time, you will keep yourself accountable just as you would maintain a ledger of financial assets. You will prioritise activities so that you live your life to the fullest. It is important to question yourself on the amount of your life's time you give to your employer. You compromise your family, your hobbies and the most valuable resource – your bag of coins. Is it worth spending your gold coins? What returns are you getting for your years of service?

Think of the work that you do: Does it fuel your passion? Does it bring you energy and a sense of fulfilment and accomplishment? Will it lead to growth or keep you stagnant? This approach will make you a decision maker and you will stop acting defensive.

Somehow, South Asian culture has lost respect for time. People feel proud to turn up late for gatherings. It gives them a sense of importance. If one out of many people turns up on time, it is believed that he has nothing important to do in life. Our moral standards have been reversed. It is likely that people who do not value their own time tend to waste the time of others, and moreover, they do not regret how conveniently and shamelessly they are stealing someone's valuable asset.

In South Asian culture, tangible things are always more valuable than intangible ones. This might be because developing countries lack material resources, and naturally in times of scarcity one will accumulate more of these resources out of fear of incapacity to afford them later. Therefore, hoarding and accumulation of goods for a rainy day is a common practice in the culture. Furthermore, large amounts of time and energy are spent in the preservation and maintenance of goods. If the preservation is eco-friendly, it makes sense; but if preservation is for an entire lifetime, such as tea sets and dinner sets that adorn dining cabinets for three decades, what is the purpose of such utensils that are hardly utilised?

It is often the case that we spend a lot of time to save a few bucks running from one store to another, from one mall to another in order to get a good bargain. But have you ever questioned how much time do you pay in order to get a good bargain? Sometimes you burn more fuel than the discount you get for which you also risk your time and energy. If that time and effort could be invested in something higher in purpose, it would exponentially multiply the amount that was to be secured in the first place getting the best bargain. Also, if you stop the preservation and hoarding of goods and money, the economy would thrive from the increased cash flow. It is understandable that past generations had been through some large financial crises and that's how they adopted such habits, but it is wise that we change habits with changing times.

Addictions – Self-Robbery

Have you ever robbed your own self? Addictions are an excellent way to do this. They steal your time without giving you anything good in return.

The question then arises, why are you okay with this robbery? You fall into an addiction in moments of hopelessness and depression. You are unable to see the silver lining and thus indulge in an activity that can make you lose consciousness of your time and space. It is the easiest way to distract yourself from feelings of anxiety and despair. But is an addiction worth having? What is the cost for overindulgence or the excess of anything – whether it is alcohol or swiping across your mobile screen? You compromise the balance in your life! You – the one who had once aspired to reach the skies – land into a pit of unrealised dreams, go astray and lose focus from your purpose. You find yourself in an unfulfilled life with a false sense of inner peace. Anything that costs you your inner balance is not worth keeping!

The ideal way to manage your time is to go with the universe and its pattern. To rise with the sun and set with it too. This is how your biological clock is naturally synchronised as long as you don't break the pattern. Only human beings have been given the power to choose and go against the pattern when all other creations, may it be plants or animals or celestial bodies, all follow the natural order. Those who do not go with the flow of the natural pattern land themselves into difficulty. Late-night sit-ins at cafes and sleeping late and consequently skipping the early sun and a morning walk will gradually take a toll on your health. The late opening hours of markets, shops and other businesses or spending the day lazing away are not the ways of progressive nations. Neither has any person ever transcended nor has any nation ever risen by wasting resources extravagantly from the national time bank.

Time Management and the Shield Against Procrastination

Time management is a skill that can only be learnt if you have internalised the value of time. If you have any doubts, you will learn procrastination instead. However, procrastination can be easily tackled if you believe you are accountable for every second you spend. The firmer the belief, the stronger the possibility of doing your tasks in time and not delaying them till the last minute. The belief in accountability in the afterlife and performing prayers five times daily are the secret sauce to managing your time efficiently.

Question yourself on the cost you have to pay when you procrastinate and delay work. It will give you a clearer vision and motivation to not procrastinate. For example, take the cost you have to pay if you have to go to a social event or business meeting and you keep delaying till the last moment. People who procrastinate are not proactive; they neither plan ahead of time nor think of upcoming challenges. Therefore, the anxiety that pushes you to do something does not build until the last hour. You might be lazing in front of the screen until the last minute; then you finally get up and search for your clothing. Now with a very short amount of time at hand, you are in a rush and the anxiety that has just built will rise exponentially. The hour that could have been a relaxing one becomes an hour of crisis wherein your brain is working beyond its capacity to squeeze everything into that hour. What if there is a power cut as you get ready or if there is too much traffic on your way? All your effort of that awesome presentation that you had planned on delivering will be overshadowed by your efforts to reach on time. Unforeseen circumstances can occur at any time, but this event was not unforeseen. If you keep a buffer of such delays by being proactive, you can save yourself the anxiety and embarrassment. You could be late by accident once or twice, but if being late becomes the norm for you, no amount of excuses can save you from being labelled or judged.

What is the best way to be proactive and stop procrastination? If you break down your tasks in smaller chunks and set shorter deadlines for each chunk, it will tune your brain to build the optimum anxiety needed for you to work – which usually, in the case of procrastinators, only mounts the last hour. Does this ring a bell for the five daily prayers? Did you ever question why you need to submit to God five times and why once a day is not enough? Breaking prayers into five chunks with deadlines and accountability stops procrastination.

If you reflect on the structure of the five prayers, you will notice that every prayer and the time duration in which it has to be offered serve a very important purpose. The dawn and dusk prayers have a very short span. The afternoon and night prayers have the longest, and the middle prayer has a suitable duration. In winters, the night prayer duration is extended, and afternoon prayer duration is shortened because of shorter days and longer nights and in summers it is vice versa.

Now think about your tasks and put them on a priority list. Some of them will be urgent and will have shorter deadlines like a customer query about the sales product. You cannot leave the customer hanging while you work on product inventory or internal documentation. You will have to respond to him immediately before he jumps to your competitor.

The prayer timings and their duration train your body and brain to act in your everyday life according to the situations and their needs. Most people are unable to prioritise their responsibilities, which lands them into tough situations where they overcommit and are unable to decide which task to tackle first. In such a case, prayers come to your rescue by training you to prioritise your tasks. As prayers are obligatory, missing them is a big sin. Hence, prioritising prayers in your daily lives teaches you how to prioritise your work based on importance and urgency. This resonates with the Eisenhower Decision Matrix. This matrix explains the similar philosophy where the tasks are divided into four quadrants. The first quadrant are the tasks that you prioritize based on importance and urgency, and in the second quadrant are the tasks that are important but not urgent.

Eisenhower Decision Matrix

	URGENT	NOT URGENT
IMPORTANT	**DO** Do it now. Write article for today.	**DECIDE** Schedule a time to do it. Exercising. Calling family and friends. Researching articles. Long-term biz strategy.
NOT IMPORTANT	**DELEGATE** Who can do it for you? Scheduling interviews. Booking flights. Approving comments. Answering certain emails. Sharing articles.	**DELETE** Eliminate it. Watching television. Checking social media. Sorting through junk mail.

In order for you to be productive you will have to stop the activities that fall in the third or fourth quadrant of the matrix. You will have to either delegate or delete those tasks. It is very similar to when you leave the work you're doing and join the congregation; it trains you to pause and pray. Not only does it make you more productive in your day-to-day tasks, it also makes it easier for you to stop, delegate or delete your current activities and fully focus on tasks of high importance and urgency.

You may have noticed that some people get so immersed in their work that they lose sense of time. This does not allow them to multitask. However, in daily life, many things require multitasking, and who better can understand the importance of multitasking than your family's Chief Executive Officer – that is, the housewife or homemaker? The way she has to manage risks and take decisions on multiple tasks in a limited time requires a great amount of skills. However, it is not easy for the brain. You need to train your brain to simultaneously perform multiple tasks without losing efficiency. Similar to the structure of how your brain works, the operating system of the computer's CPU is designed to pipeline and parallel process its background and foreground operations.

You might be wondering what it has to do with performing prayers. Have you ever questioned why there is *Rakah* (unit) count in every prayer? It is to break your focus and immersion in prayer, if there is one, or from the train of thoughts that come one after another like that of the story build-up of the next episode of GOT, and bring your consciousness back so that you can keep count. Keeping and remembering the unit count trains your brain not only in prayer but in life outside as well – to dissociate yourself from your current task and become conscious of your surroundings.

You may be wondering that although maintaining focus is essential – in both prayer and life outside – breaking the concentration is unheard of. There could be an unforeseen danger in your surroundings, a risk to your own life or an emergency that needs immediate attention, like a baby who is about to reach for a glass vase. You will not sense the danger if you remain immersed in worship for a long time without breaking focus. Therefore, it is prohibited to pray with closed eyes. And as for life outside the prayers, remembering to turn off the stove while you are immersed in a book can save you from potential danger.

> *"So, woe to those who pray. [But] who are heedless of their prayer."*
> *– (Quran 107:4-5)*

Allah in 'Surah Al Ma'un' has cursed people who despite praying are not conscious of their prayers. Allah, the most Compassionate, has put so much emphasis on the importance of performing this ritual soulfully. He is the Creator of the entire universe and has power over everything, if He intends destruction for you who then can guarantee you success? Just imagine how lethal procrastination is in leading a goal-oriented life and how proactivity ensures self-actualisation.

These are timeless teachings, which, if applied in the right way, will teach you time management and work–life balance that you aim to have in your life.

Here is the secret: Once you understand the value of time, stop wasting yours as well as the time of others and be conscious of where you are spending it, Allah will make you valuable. Every minute of yours will be highly worthy. Your net worth will increase both financially and socially as people will value your presence and time. You will realise your dreams and become a self-actualised person.

Summary

- Discover your strengths and weaknesses, which will help you find your purpose.
- Respect your time by utilising it purposefully. Also, do not rob others of their most valuable asset.
- Prayers help you in overcoming procrastination and becoming proactive. They help you to be focussed while at the same time staying aware of your surroundings.

- Prioritise your tasks so as to make optimum use of time.
- In order to manage time effectively, go with the natural pattern of the universe.
- In order to be proactive and well organised, maintain a scheduling calendar. Also, use time off applications on your devices for a time-out from technology.

Chapter Six

The Motivational Fuel

Mastering Emotions

Emotions play a significant role in a human being. They act like a barometer that indicates your level of inner peace. The first signs of anger, disappointment or anxiety signal that there is something wrong in your environment or external self which is not in tune with your inner self. This disrupts your peace and motivates you to take an action that is usually overt in your behaviour.

For example, if you see a wild animal in your surroundings, you will instantly feel a sense of fear, which will compel you to look for shelter and save yourself. Just imagine, if there was no sense of fear, you would have easily become a feast for the beast. So, emotions CAN be your saviour, provided you use them intelligently.

Take another instance: you worked really hard to grow your business; somewhere along the journey you faced a setback, you lost hope and gave up your struggle because you were overcome by the fear of failure.

Now just for a moment think. What made you associate the emotion of fear with that wild animal? And how did you associate fear with your failure? There are two things that play an active role in building your perceptions: your natural disposition and your environment. Even if no one told you that the wild animal is dangerous, you will feel a physical reaction from within in the form of nervousness or goosebumps that will signal you to save yourself. At the same time, a child that has not been told how harmful that beast can be does not perceive it as dangerous, because his brain has not developed enough to respond to his natural disposition. Therefore, he will not feel the fear or the need to escape. In this time period while his brain is still growing, if you make him believe that the animal's wild expressions are harmless and an expression of love, what will happen? It will override his natural instinct because of what he has been conditioned to believe. This would result in loss of life with his next encounter with the wild beast even if that happens later in his adulthood.

Now get back to the scenario where you faced a major setback in the business and gave up. How did you associate the emotion of fear with failure? Who told you to feel fear when you fail? From where did you learn this notion? Did someone in your environment discourage you whenever you tried and failed in it? Did someone shame you or criticise you? Did someone embarrass you for not scoring good enough in your examinations? Often this attitude of criticism and discouragement is a part of your everyday expressions. Critical comments can be 'Loser, what a failure!' or 'He is a total disappointment!'

The way you perceive your failures define the emotions that you feel. Similarly, the way you perceive negative experiences of bullying, criticism or labels define the emotions that you feel.

Let's return to the good and bad usage of your emotional signals: taking action by perceiving a wild animal to be dangerous and feeling fear is a positive emotion and a primary need for our survival, but giving up trying by perceiving a failure to be an ultimate loss and feeling fear is a negative emotion. The emotion of fear is the same but gives two different results, and the very same emotion can be positive in one situation and negative in another. It is up to you how you utilise your emotions!

Having said that, it's not only about you utilising your emotions; people too can exploit them and control you through manipulation. The most common example of control is when a caregiver uses the emotion of fear to control a child and make him listen. It is definitely a shortcut to make someone obey. Why only children, even societies are kept under fear so as to control the crowd. For achieving this emotion, even a rumour can do the job! Islamophobia in this case is a very relevant example. Using the media houses strategically, fear is ingrained in the minds of common people. This is such an effective way of gaining control over public by creating a rift so much so that people have started doubting their decade-old neighbours and childhood friends just because they belong to a certain faith and dress in a certain way.

It is so unfortunate that we instil the fear of Allah in our children instead of instilling His love. The first introduction that Allah has given about Himself is that of *Ar-Rahman – Ar-Raheem* (The Entirely Merciful, the Especially Merciful), and what first impression do we give of Him to our children? In order that children pray on time or speak the truth or obey us, we have a shortcut to make them listen and take quick action. We make our children fear Allah as if He is a Being who is always there to throw them in hellfire whenever they do not conform!

Not only this, fear is an important ingredient in marketing and advertising too. Come on, buy the promo tickets before they are sold out or a cotton or lawn seller will make you fear the limited stocks that are running out. You – out of FOMO (Fear Of Missing Out) – will stock up dresses way beyond your need. The dollar prices can go up and down by instilling a similar fear. If you are not self-aware, you will easily flow with the emotions, internalising the feelings that others want you to feel and displaying them in your behaviour and thus ruining yourself.

You may often get demoralised, upset or disappointed by how badly people behave with you. You have a choice to either keep complaining about their bad attitude, or treat it as an opportunity for growth.

Unfortunately, we live in a polar society that believes in extremes, and so we feel intense emotions. We know how to behave, react and communicate as a reaction to these intense emotions. For example, we have many examples of behaviours, patterns and vocabulary to use when we are angry, but we literally need to create new behaviours and vocabulary to express when we're slightly upset, so as to convey our message without getting aggressive. We know exactly how to disapprove and criticise others, but we struggle to offer constructive feedback. Hence, there's a lack of positive vocabulary in our language of expression. We are also very used to the intensity and extremity, and hence we don't care to lend our ear unless the emotional temperatures soar higher. We are miserly in appreciating others because we think they will be on cloud nine if we do so (another extreme assumption or behaviour). We need to transform our vocabulary using modifiers to soften the intensity of our emotions.

For example:
Destroyed -> setback
Confused -> curious
Afraid -> uncomfortable
Hate -> prefer
Lost -> searching
Frustrated -> challenged
Stupid -> learning

Now let me show you the different ways in which people can exploit your emotions through their negative behaviours and how you can give these emotions a new meaning so that they become a fuel for your motivation, empowering you to reach your higher purpose and goals.

The first step is to fully accept the emotion you are feeling. Accept your anger, jealousy, guilt, frustration, boredom and so forth. It is okay to feel what you are feeling. The problem arises when you internalise your feelings deep down with a NEGATIVE meaning and display it in the form of a negative reaction. Never try to suppress it, because it will lead to a state of denial of a potential problem that might be disrupting your inner peace that you are not willing to confront.

Manipulating Emotions

Human nature is designed on the principle of being motivated to do something either to avoid pain or to gain pleasure. Your motivation to buy a particular brand of laptop out of so many others is that extra wireless headset you are getting along with it, thereby increasing your pleasure and ease of communication. On the other hand, you are motivated to submit your assignment on time without missing the deadline in order to avoid the pain to resubmit another one in case it is not accepted due to late submission. In short, you are motivated either by love or by fear or loss. Depending on your interests and priorities, in some areas, you will get easily motivated by love whereas, in other areas of life, you will need a fear-based strategy so that you are accountable for your responsibilities. The concept of heaven and hell in the spiritual world works on the same pleasure or pain principle: there are moments in your life when you are so motivated to be the best version of yourself, fulfilling your responsibilities for the love and blessings you may get from Allah and the perfect permanent abode in the form of heaven; while, there are times in your life that only a reminder of a painful consequence in the form of hell and its everlasting punishment can push you out of bed to maintain the necessary balance that you need in life in order to have a more meaningful and impactful existence.

Take the example of this couple who used to fight day in and day out. The wife would take her own sweet time to dress up while the husband would wait in the car. Every other outing, they would plan would start with a bad mood on both sides. Only if the husband is able to find out the right key to motivate her in being quick, they can find a solution to their persistent fights.

The key is to identify the type of motivation as it varies from person to person and situation to situation. You must have noticed how retail companies motivate buyers to shop from their store by running sale promotions of 'buy one get one free' or 50% off. They make sure they attract both kinds of buyers – the one that finds pleasure in gaining that extra pack of socks and the other that finds pleasure by avoiding the pain of spending the full amount for socks that they can get at half price.

Redefining Negativity

Now that we have understood the concept of how emotions act as signals and how motivation is driven from pain or pleasure, can you ascribe meaning and different emotions to a situation that is demoralising and to a situation that motivates you by either bringing in the emotions of pleasure or avoiding pain? How about redefining criticisms, judgements, comparisons and jealousies and giving them a new meaning, deriving an entirely different emotion that fuels your motivation? Instead of falling back, you will keep moving forward regardless of how much negativity is present in your surroundings, turning it into a frictional force that keeps pushing you forward.

Criticisms are often categorised as constructive or destructive, but there is nothing as such. Either it is criticism or it is feedback, because both have an entirely different intention and way of communicating the message. Feedback is meant for your improvements and is communicated in a way that encourages you to put in your best efforts and motivate you to keep trying, while criticism is a shot of negative energy fired on you, with the intention of humiliating you – which if internalised can ruin your self-esteem and confidence. Not everyone in this world is here to lift you. You will encounter people who will be driven by jealousy and complexes and enjoy feeling superior by putting you down. If you get dragged into their drama, you will enter the negative zone. You will damage your self-image and lose your self-worth. In this process, you will shatter your confidence and stop believing in your potential.

Here, I will tell you a secret that will empower you not only to avoid being the part of their circus but will also help you generate motivation fuel from their negative energy. And it is very easy! You just have to give a different meaning to their criticism and derive pleasure through your accomplishment – everything else will fall into place.

Consider this situation: you are in a position of leadership where you are criticised for your actions. No matter what you do, it is seen from a critical lens; you are labelled and judged for your every action in both your public and private life. How you define this experience will dictate the course of your action. If you associate emotions of self-doubt, worthlessness and not being good enough to this negative experience or become angry at every bark, chances are you will get stuck and demotivated.

> *'The story you tell yourself becomes your inner voice.'*

What if you define their harsh comments as challenges or targets for yourself *if* they are worth achieving? Once you achieve this and your achievements contradict their proclamations, they will have to take their words back. You will gain pleasure by feeling accomplished and fulfilled, deriving positive emotions from the negative energy that was thrown at you and giving new meaning to the negative experience. Instead of being stuck or demotivated by the negativity, you use it to fuel your motivation to reach higher and higher and excel in your journey.

> *'If you are irritated by every rub, how will you become polished?'*
> *– Rumi*

However, it is important to make sure you are setting a target worthy of yourself and not being used by becoming a puppet to their negative aspirations. I had a client who was often rubbed the wrong way by others' negative comments and kept striving to prove otherwise. All his energy was consumed in proving that he was a better son, a better husband, a more loyal friend, a better father or a better colleague than what people said he was. He no longer had energy left to dive into his own self, reflect upon his personal passions and goals in life. He was so busy proving himself to others that he did not find the time or energy to look himself in the mirror and stop judging himself from the eyes of others. Passive-aggressive people manipulate you, drain your energy and drag you into their negative space. Build healthy boundaries so that you don't give in to their demands and expectations. It is a sad reality, but people who manipulate you are often the people that you love the most. They emotionally blackmail you to work on their agenda. If you are self-aware and do not let the emotions do a power play, you will not only rediscover yourself but also empower the other persons to rediscover their lost self and aspirations that they are trying to seek through you.

There are also many people who are not socially intelligent enough to give friendly feedback. They have only learnt to use a negative tone to offer the best feedback, which could give you a different perspective overcoming your blind spots. This valuable information could widen your intelligence and prove to be a turning point. Your declining business, your quality of work or your relationships can highly improve if you lend an ear and overlook their tone of voice or style of communication. The key is to identify your emotions when you encounter such people. Accept your frustration and anger, but before you are overpowered by these feelings – which could become visible in your expressions or behaviour – quickly give them a new meaning that serves you and does not drain your energy. Analyse the labels, criticisms and comments from an unbiased and non-defensive attitude. Pick the good from it and the possibilities that could help you grow, and work on them to be even better than before. The moment you are able to do so, you will be in charge of your emotions. You will feel the way you want to feel at that moment, the thoughts you want to think and the actions you want to take rather than being swayed by the negative pull.

People judge. Human beings are judgmental, and this is what distinguishes them from other creations. Human beings use their judgement to differentiate right from wrong and for self-evaluation. The problem arises when you use the power of judgement not to evaluate and reflect on your own discrepancies, but to evaluate others and boost your own ego.

People might give you different labels based on their perceptions. Every word has a positive and negative meaning. Try fitting a device in your brain that converts all negative **labels** into positive ones, so all you hear when people call you bossy is 'leader'; if people call you stubborn you hear 'dedicated'; if people call you attention seeker you hear 'irresistible' and if people call you a coaxer you hear 'influential'. By converting your pain into pleasure, you are able to stop the negative thoughts that these labels are supposed to generate.

However, there will be moments when you are not having a good day, and you could lose your temper – it is okay. Don't try to be a perfectionist. Remind yourself that you are always on a learning curve, a work in progress. Don't be hard on yourself; do not become a victim of the situation. In fact, learn from the situation and recognise the cues that irritate you enough to lose control. Identify these cues so that the next time when you feel them in your surroundings, you are proactive in deciding what is the best action you can take.

Social comparisons are a way to show disappointments and make people feel bad about themselves. They silently cut the roots of any relationship because you are never good enough; there is always somebody better than you who will be brought in comparison to show how unworthy you are.

When you compare your child's potential with that of his cousin or classmate, you are not only making him feel unworthy, but you are also instilling in him feelings of jealousy and stubbornness by not accepting his own uniqueness. Education is a means of personal growth and excellence, and competition fuels jealousy. When a wife always complains to her husband about how her sister's husband brings flowers for her on every occasion, she is not valuing what her husband does for her, and when a husband compares his wife to his mother and sister, it is a sign of ingratitude in the relationship.

Then there are some people who are great at **gaslighting**. They will make every attempt to fuel your anger while maintaining their composure.

Losing emotions in such situations will make you vulnerable and exposed. To shut them up, politely let them know that you are a work in progress and are in no way perfect, and that you value their constructive feedback. In this way, you help diffuse their negativity and remain in your safe zone without bringing the worst out of you.

Strong people master their emotions and maintain the calm in them.

You will encounter people who use you as a mirror of their own deficiencies and complexes. They will lead a life of self-denial, and the only time they will face their shortcomings is when they will look at themselves through you, by projecting their flaws and weaknesses as yours. For example, a husband who is hostile in nature and has anger-management issues would blame his wife for being hostile, or a husband who is cheating on his wife would 'project' his behaviour on his wife – out of guilt and internal conflict – and accuse her of having an affair. A parent who finds it difficult to have a work-life balance can project his guilt of not spending quality time with the kids by blaming them to be careless and inconsiderate. A manager who is not capable of making good predictions and is unable to make critical decisions will shift the blame onto his team at the time of crisis.

People use **projections** as a self-defence mechanism so that the blame of their own weakness is put on others and they can easily escape from the situation. If you happen to encounter such people, the best strategy is not to internalise their criticisms. Accept your emotions and master them. Feelings of self-confidence, knowing your self-worth and not seeking validation of yourself through their lens will help you avoid the pain they are trying to inflict upon you, through their projections. Being grateful for not being in their situation will help you sympathise their condition and overcome their negativity. For example, a self-talk that will endorse your qualities and a positive self-image will give new meaning to this experience, acting as a shield that will re-bounce their flaws back on to them. Sympathise with their internal state of guilt and dissatisfaction. When you stop accepting their blame and quietly walk away from their drama, they will stop projecting their negative attributes onto you. If you accept the accusations, they will continue to play as it will give them a sense of satisfaction for their restless and internally conflicted self. You would have provided them a way to excuse them of their personal flaws and the cycle will continue.

There are times when you will feel jealous. **Jealousy** is an emotion; therefore, it is a signal trying to give you some message. Take the message and let go off the emotion. If you see someone making progress and you sense jealousy within you, what do you think this emotion is trying to convey? You feel jealous when you have inner emptiness – some passion, a purpose yet to be discovered. When you see the other person progressing, there is a cry from inside that is telling you to pursue your dreams, explore your passions. If you use this jealousy as a meaningful emotion, an emotion that pushes you out of your comfort zone and motivates you to take action towards your personal goals, this emotion is positive. It will become negative if you become the victim of your situation and desire affliction and distress on those who have progressed more than you.

You will come across people who are good at **ghosting**. Without any explanation they will leave you in the middle of a relationship, making you wonder what went wrong. Silent treatment, being used and disposed of, feelings of rejection and low self-esteem might cripple you further. But by now, you have already mastered your emotions and know how to navigate these feelings and redefine them to a deeper level to understand how people are unable to confront their emotional discomfort and passively withdraw from relationships. You become an observer and not a victim, and can easily sympathise with their immaturity in relationships and incapability of handling conflicts in a healthier way.

People often criticise your uniqueness; since you are unlike them, it is difficult for them to accept your individuality. Value yourself, and they will eventually start valuing you.

People will motivate you only till the time they believe you to be below them. Once they see you outgrow them, they will feel insecure. Keep going and you will turn into their inspiration.

Summary

- Identify the reason behind feeling a particular way. This will help you master your emotions and utilise them in better ways.
- Find what drives your motivation so that you can manipulate your emotions to take the desired actions.
- Give new meaning to all the negativity that is thrown towards you and make it your motivational fuel to accelerate your pace of reaching greater heights.

Chapter Seven

Striking Balance

There was a boy who would rub his skin whenever a mosquito bit him. The skin would become sore. He could not resist the urge to scratch his skin whenever he felt the tingling sensation because of the bite. His mum told him that the mosquito bite was a lesson to teach him patience. If he could learn the lesson in the simplest way by resisting the urge to scratch and letting it heal, it would be good for him. Otherwise, the lesson would keep repeating itself, throughout the kid's life, but in more severe ways so as to empower him with patience.

In the last chapter, we discussed the negative behaviours of others that can trigger an emotionally unstable response in you. By manipulating your emotions and giving those behaviours a different meaning, you can fuse out the negativity they contain; but often everything happens in a flash and you don't get time to think and process. In this chapter, you will learn the tools needed to accelerate the process of balancing out the negative energy so that you do not swirl in the vicious circle of negativity. Moreover, these tools will help you attract positive energies so that you become empowered and resourceful, which acts as a shield against negative behaviours generated either externally by others/your environment or from within.

Consider this situation. You are running a small group of people sharing a common interest. You plan events and activities for the group and put in a lot of time and effort to execute them in the best possible manner with the available resources at hand. Many people will appreciate your work and encourage you, but there will be a few naysayers. Their role in the community is nothing more than to offer criticism and disapproval. If they happen to contribute financially, they will nudge you from time to time questioning you about their petty contribution. If you happen to encounter a naysayer at a critical moment where you are overly exhausted, chances are you might lose your temper and get provoked to react by the negativity. It is this very moment that patience, if exercised, becomes your powerful shield and saves you from any form of embarrassment or humiliation that you may regret later.

Patience – Action and Not Reaction

It is very important to understand what patience actually is, because we confuse it with many other things that it is not. Patience is controlling your urge to react to your negative emotions and controlling your desire to respond despite having the power to do so. For example, your spouse compares you with so and so and tries to belittle you. This will instantly build negative thoughts in you, and your emotion will signal the discomfort you just felt by his offense. Patience in such a situation is the self-restraint that empowers you to pull yourself away from the negativity that is fired on you, so that you are not dragged into the drama whose stage has already been set.

It is easier said than done because in the heat of the moment it is very difficult to hold yourself from giving a reaction. Patience enables you to buy time to act than to react, helping you to practise the pause and reflect on your emotions, thus channelising them productively, communicating your concerns and defending yourself more effectively.

Everyone has the right to defend themselves. Patience helps you analyse the situation first before stepping in and utilising your energy in diffusing the negativity instead of further igniting it.

What if someone knows exactly where and how to press your buttons? And what if you give in to his tactics?

Avoid confronting such a person and occupy yourself elsewhere. If you can't avoid the person or situation, don't internalise his words or behaviour.

Accept your emotions. Give yourself time to think; analyse and re-evaluate the situation that went wrong; utilise that feedback to improve next time.

The Need for Patience

In today's world, where all your needs are fulfilled by just a swipe of your mobile screen, you literally don't have to move an inch to get things done. One cannot deny the advantages of technology, but at the same time, if it is used to make things easier, it makes us impatient. When you interact with each other through screens, you lose out on the social and emotional intelligence that you learn from face-to-face interactions. Without this intelligence, you become very focussed and self-centred in meeting your needs without having to wait.

For example, ordering food online takes away your experience of actually visiting the restaurant, interacting with people, standing in a queue and waiting for your turn to get your meal. Instant gratification is another issue that gives rise to spontaneous actions and frustration if your expectations are not being met. Video games teach children that they will get instant gains and rewards without having to make much effort.

Parents exercise instant gratification too when they boss their children around to listen and act on their commands without giving them sufficient time to process the instructions and disconnect from their present activity. If you raise your voice when you do not get an instant response, you are being impatient. And you are also teaching your child to do the same.

Similarly, a lack of patience cannot make you a good teacher or even a preacher. In order for you to have effective communication and make the person understand your point of view, you need to be an active listener. Active listening requires a lot of patience. You will feel the desire to negate an erroneous statement, but you need to be wise enough to wait and hold back your desire to interrupt. Listen to the other party completely, empathise and reach his level in order to communicate and teach him a different perspective.

There are so many challenging situations in your daily life that can either frustrate you or can be an opportunity to build powerful memories. Situations like being stuck in traffic, waiting in long queues, surviving summer heat or winter chills – anything beyond your circle of influence – can either fill your bank of negative energy or empower you.

Consider this. You have planned a movie with your spouse and it's getting late. Your spouse takes a lot of time to get ready. Either you grumble all the way, honking and rushing to reach the cinema, or you let go, take a deep breath and enjoy the moment. The choice is yours. In any case, making your spouse conform to your needs is beyond your circle of influence. Strong marital relationships require a lot of compassion and patience in understanding each other's needs. Criticism and grumbling are certainly not ways to show compassion and patience. You need to learn ways of communicating your needs more effectively.

How to Be Patient?

Patience empowers you to be in a more resourceful state. During testing times, you often hear people advising you to be patient, but rarely does anyone teach you how to be patient, and unless you know how to, how are you going to be patient? You need to learn the tools and techniques on how to foster patience.

Below are some techniques that can help you exercise patience effectively.

- **Managing the Emotional States**

It is often difficult to hide your feelings from others when you are irritated or annoyed by them or by an unfavourable situation. Before you can even ascribe new meaning to it, your body reacts to the negativity. Giving an instant reaction will not only expose you but also prove to them that their tactic to demean you actually worked.

Some people let anger brew inside them long enough until the volcano of unmanaged emotions bursts at the wrong place and time. They lose their sanity and this sudden outburst of negative emotions goes against them. Despite being right, others perceive them as the problem makers. There is no use regretting the arrow that has already left the bow. You should be well prepared to handle any kind of negativity that is thrown at you and should not give a spontaneous or incoherent reaction.

In order for you to not lose your composure, it is necessary that you manage your emotional state. There are two ways to do this:

- Change your focus – Distract yourself from the situation or thoughts that come along by pushing yourself to think about something else. *Dhikr (Arabic word which means* remembering God by repetitive recitation of divine words) is a way to distract yourself from the negativity by diverting your brain to recite divine words that cleanse your negativity with their power. My favourite *dhikr* at a time when I need to exercise patience is

    'Indeed, Allah is with the patient.'
    and
    'Allah is sufficient for me. There is no God but Him, I put my trust in Him and He is the Lord of the great heavens.'

These words give me the assurance that I am not alone and someone bigger than me is taking care of my affairs.

Another way in which you can ensure that you do not internalise critical comments thrown at you is to keep on repeating to yourself: '*Not my monkeys, not my circus!*' This mantra will help you to not associate yourself with the mess that other people are involved in.

But if you are a person who is very focused and cannot be easily distracted, the second trick might work for you.

- Change your physiology – You can change your emotional state by changing your physical state. If you are angry, fake a smile until you make it. Or change your posture: if you are sitting, move around; if you are standing, take a deep breath and sit down. Usually, when we are under intense emotions, our body temperature shoots up. Drink water or splash some onto your face to lower your body temperature. By changing your physical state, you will be able to manage your emotional state. This will ensure you do not give unwanted reactions that may later prove an embarrassment for you.

Both of these strategies of managing emotional states are the *sunnah* of the Prophet ﷺ. Indeed, the Prophetic wisdom gives us the guidance to manage our negative states effectively.

- **Learning to Wait and Delayed Gratification**

You should always give your children a time span during which they choose to run a particular errand. Give them a grace period if a certain task is not done within time. Model the behaviour that you want to see in your child. Wait before your request is serviced.

For example, if you want your child to clean up his room, ask him what is the best time that he can he do it. Instead of showing authority, teach him to be responsible by giving him the choice. He will learn to take decisions and also learn the importance of commitment rather than being taught to take orders. Hold him accountable for his commitments. Let him take ownership of his actions. Reward him for fulfilling his commitments or take away privileges if he does not do what he says he will. If you reward him for taking orders and submitting to your wishes, it will only foster conditional love and not integrity. Conditional love leads to people-pleasing behaviour. However, you will require a lot of energy and patience to be able to do this.

Delayed gratification is a technique that builds *self-control* and *patience*. The Stanford marshmallow experiment was a series of studies on delayed gratification in the late 1960s and early 1970s led by psychologist Walter Mischel, then professor at Stanford University. In these studies, a child was offered a choice between one small reward provided immediately or two small rewards if he waited for a short period, approximately 15 minutes, during which the tester left the room and then returned. In follow-up studies, the researchers found that children who were able to wait longer for the preferred rewards tended to have better life outcomes, as measured by SAT scores, educational attainment, body mass index (BMI) and other life measures.

I remember when my elder brother was in boarding school, we used to drop him to the bus stand where families of other kids would gather to see them off. While my parents would network with other families and my brother would be excited about being united with his school friends, I would sit idle for hours in the car waiting for the bus to leave. My dad, just like me, had problems letting go, and hence we were the last ones to leave at wedding functions, family gatherings or at the airport seeing our relatives off until the aeroplane finally flew. As a child with no technology to pass time, those were testing times for me. I guess the reason behind my love for books is that I have waited a lot in my life, and in order to make that wait pleasurable, books always kept me a good company. How bitter those experiences felt at that time; but I realised, with time, that every experience – good or bad – served me in some way. It instilled in me tolerance, self-control and the ability to wait.

I thought about trying the same experiment with my ten-year-old boy who is crazy about a particular chocolate dessert at Chilli's. Whenever he sees that molten lava cake in front of him, he loses control, forgets table etiquette and starts devouring it as if it is the first and the last time he will ever eat it! When we are sharing this dessert, he does not even stop to care about the others who should get their share. One day, we leisurely walked into the restaurant and after having our main meal ordered the chocolate dessert. Before they served us, I challenged my son whether he could resist his gluttony and have two small spoons of it after which he would sit back and let others enjoy his favourite dessert. My son agreed to the plan. He had two spoons and sat silently watching us eat. He had just made a memory for a lifetime. Just as for me, the memory of those long waits gives me power in my testing times, this memory of controlling himself from his most favourite food empowered him. One day I was bribing him to do something and offered a chocolate puff as a reward, to which he said if he could resist the molten lava cake, this was nothing in comparison to that! The experiment backfired on me in the most beautiful way because I knew then that if someone bribed him later in his life for personal gains, he had a powerful memory that would stop him from falling for it.

Fasting is an alternative way of practising delayed gratification. The concept of heaven and hell also teaches you self-control: you have to control your instincts and desires and not let them loose in order to gain a place in heaven, where all desires are fulfilled, or hell, which warns you of the negative consequences if you go overboard and lose the balance. Unfortunately, fasting has become feasting and more of a tradition than an exercise to build self-control.

Difference Between Patience, Endurance and Forbearance

The memory of my long waits is powerful if I use it intelligently. If I use it to let go and tolerate too much, people will step over my boundaries. Therefore, patience is often confused with forbearance and endurance. Many times, society misinterprets patience and advises people to be patient in times when they actually need support to speak up and act. Imagine situations where people are oppressed and they are advised to be patient – do they actually have a choice whether to react or not? Such people endure oppression not out of choice but out of helplessness and lack of power. These are people that you need to support and stand up on their behalf, to speak up against oppression and injustice, instead of redefining their forced silence as patience and commemorating it as a holy act.

For example, when a woman is emotionally or physically abused in a marital relationship – instead of speaking out on the injustice that her marriage has led to and strengthen her by supporting her in bettering her situation, we honour her powerlessness and vulnerability as an act of bravery and celebrate her suffering as heroic and inspirational for other women to follow.

The Arabic words *Sabr* and *Tahammul* are two different terms with entirely different meanings. *Tahammaul* has roots in the word *haml*, which means to carry a burden. For example, when things don't go right or someone else does wrong, holding back from reacting is patience and excusing them for their behaviour is *tahammul* or forbearance. Forbearance is the willingness to carry the burden of their wrong and bear the consequence of their action without showing discomfort. In order to forbear, one needs to have a lot of compassion. The forbearance our Prophet showed for the lady who threw garbage over him was because of the compassion he had for humanity, and it was because of this compassion that she later embraced Islam.

A mother often forbears her children out of maternal love and excuses them for their unreasonable behaviour. Blood relations have the capability to forbear out of compassionate bonds. It is for this reason that no matter how intensely siblings may fight, at the end of the day they are able to forgive and forget. They can have all kind of justifications to excuse each other for their mistakes.

Sabr in many cases is followed or accompanied by forbearance; hence they are mistakenly used interchangeably. However, a very fine line distinguishes them. For example, in the case of a sibling fight, you might not be patient – that is, you do not resist the urge to react, show anger or say mean words – but finally you do display forbearance towards your sibling. For example, you and your sibling leave for college using the same mode of commute, but it is your sibling who gets ready last minute and because of this you too get late. You might not be patient and may be quick to react with mean words, but then again you willingly carry the burden of his laziness the very next day.

Forbearance – What Is the Right Balance?

Forbearance is an act of compassion not only towards others but to your own self. When you forbear the consequences of other people's mistakes, you acknowledge the human capacity to err and thus you also excuse yourself for your own human imperfections. If you let go of someone else's fault, the next time you will also be exempted from being charged on yours. It is essential to be easy on yourself and others. It is okay to be human.

However, when a mistake becomes a habit, it is then binding on you to not be stung by someone more than twice. Sometimes, too much forbearance is another extreme and teaches others to treat you like a doormat and in cases can spoil them.

People who have a greater degree of tolerance have a higher threshold before their limit of endurance is crossed. They tend to ignore the red signals where they need to react and reclaim their peace. If you are such a kind, people might exploit your tolerance and take advantage of your compassion. They are sure you will not react and will keep on carrying the burden of their ills. You set the bar for them to treat you like this. It is at this point that learning the fine balance between forbearance and holding others accountable for their wrong actions and letting them taste its consequence is very important. Sometimes, it is necessary to hold people accountable for their actions instead of letting them go in the name of forbearance, because otherwise you encourage and support their wrong actions by accepting them. This will be a heavy baggage for you to carry and will affect your self-care immensely.

The balance can be reached when we understand and internalise that the curse of an oppressed person reaches the skies swiftly and is heard by the All Hearing; therefore, one should not take advantage of a situation where an oppressed person does not speak up. On the other hand, giving ease and grace to the people who owe you in fulfilling your rights not only brings ease in your own life but also washes your sins. Therefore, we will be able to build a society where the oppressed are supported and the oppressive are punished. At the same time, we will build a society that forbears each other's imperfections so as to nurture an environment of compassion and peace.

Many people think that forbearance is equivalent to cowardice. This is not true. Sometimes, we mix forbearance with being a person who is either a doormat or an angel who gives up his own rights and wishes or as a coward who in the name of tolerance does not speak up against oppression. Often, we hush our children when they complain of injustice and bullying. We are teaching them that it is okay to bear oppression. Remember, not voicing out the wrong and presenting it as a positive attitude of forbearance is only an attempt at justifying your spinelessness. There is a fine line between defence and revenge. Teach your children to defend themselves when needed.

There was a man who loved providing ease to others. One Ramadan, a family relocated into the neighbourhood and became his next-door neighbours. He was naturally inclined to provide them ease in the scorching summer heat. He left the shared space outside his house vacant so that the movers could park the truck and unload their belongings. For a few days, he continued providing ease by parking his car elsewhere when he returned from work and walking a longer distance to his home so that his new neighbours could settle down well. After five days of adequate help, he thought about parking his car at his old parking spot. Next day on returning from work, he comfortably parked his car at the old spot. Just five minutes later, his doorbell rang, and his next-door neighbour was asking him to remove his car from the spot because he had assumed that the parking space belonged to him.

Despite having two designated parking spaces for himself within the house and the only neighbour who had the luxury of having two spaces in the whole compound, the neighbour wanted to claim the third space as an exclusive parking spot for his guests. Sometimes, favours, especially unspecified ones, end up becoming expectations and these expectations become the right.

In a society where people are always ready to take undue advantage without giving back, a time comes when the givers stop giving. The society rots because then everyone is only interested in personal gains without any pain. They become insensitive to each other's needs. To keep the cycle of positivity going, put your share in. It is not necessary to compensate each other in a similar way. Everyone is unique with different potential. Think of contributing to society keeping in mind the future of your offspring instead of a form of trade between each other. The positivity you offer into the system will make it blossom and will return to you when you need it the most.

Summary

- So that you do not regret your actions later, patience saves you from the embarrassment that comes from spontaneous reactions.
- Learn to manage and control your emotional states so that your opponent feels disappointed with his failed attempts at demoralising you.
- Learn to wait and exercise delayed gratification. This will help you to build self-control.
- Learn the right balance between patience, forbearance and endurance. Learn to differentiate between self-defence and revenge.
- Identify the line of action to take, according to the situation and circumstances. Every situation is subjective and relative; you cannot use a 'one size fits all' approach to handle them.

Chapter Eight

The Invincible You

'When memories, no matter good or bad, make you smile, know that you have become invincible.'

Hakuna Matata – It Means No Worries

Do you remember the pouch of gold coins you had on the island? They were very dear to you because they ensured your survival, and you spent each and every coin very carefully so as not to waste any of them. Imagine if someone grabs some of these coins from you and throws them in the sea. How are you going to feel? After all, it is your most valued asset! You will feel angry and helpless when you see them being thrown in the sea, right? What if I say, it was you who had mugged your own self and thrown those coins in the sea? Doesn't make sense? Why would you do that to yourself? But the truth is, you do that often! Let me show you how.

There was a man on that island who was handed a bag of coins just like you. One day, he saw a big restaurant on the island. It seemed inviting especially with pictures of those scrumptious dishes that he was craving for since days. He had to save his coins so he could not spend them lavishly, but now he felt like celebrating. He invited his friends and entered the restaurant with the bag of coins in his pocket. He ordered his most favourite and most expensive meal from the menu and impatiently awaited its arrival. As soon as the meal arrived, he could not resist and dug in to take the first bite. As soon as he did, he spat it out. The spices they used did not favour his taste buds. He requested the staff not to charge for the meal – after all, his gold coins were highly valuable! But they did not heed his request, claiming that the spices were mentioned on the menu and they too had spent from their limited bag of coins to cook his meal. Hence, they could not provide any compensation. He could not challenge them, as he had not checked out the menu properly in his hurry to get his meal. He left the restaurant disappointed. Not only had he wasted his coins but he also did not get to satisfy his cravings.

He spent the rest of his time on the island regretting his spontaneity, blaming himself for ordering the wrong dish and wasting his coins. Every other day, he would remember his mistake and how his friends enjoyed their meal, he would curse the staff for not briefing him and would hold on to his bag of coins tightly, swearing never to try any other restaurant on the island. Each day, life would claim all kinds of expenses from his bag of coins until his bag went empty. His life on the island ended. It was filled with regrets, complaints, hopelessness and disappointments, and each day his resentments robbed him of the gold coins he was left with.

In our life too, we often order that dish. We make mistakes; many times, circumstances do not favour us, or people do not support us. We see others enjoying while we are being tested. Our memories are bitter just like that oddly flavoured dish. And we waste our time recalling those memories and tasting bitterness for the rest of our life.

You must be wondering why I used the analogy of a meal. Life is harder than a meal you dislike! Our bitter past is as insignificant as that dish. It is not worth wasting your present in the resentment of past memories. Leave your past behind and live the present moment with joy and happiness – live a life without worries!

Past – A Lesson in Time

You may think that if past is that unimportant, then why are we gifted with 'memories'? Life then should be all about the present moment.

Kent Cochrane K.C. experienced a traumatic head injury in a motorcycle accident and consequently suffered from severe amnesia. He did not remember anything. Neither did he have the ability to think about the future. The only exception was the experiences that he had in the last minute or two.

Imagine a person who does not have a memory! How would he learn and live in the present when each time his only memory is of the last minute?

Nothing is created without purpose; thus, the past serves us by teaching us very important lessons. Such deep-seated lessons, especially the bitter experiences, help us improve our present. Otherwise, how would we progress if we kept repeating our old mistakes again and again?

However, sometimes, it becomes very difficult to forget the past and certain memories keep bothering you. They keep you occupied. The more you recall, the more the resentment builds.

Your surroundings, your physical and emotional environments, your associations with other humans are all a part of your human conditioning. Hence, with all this in the background, it is challenging to pull yourself out from the years of pain and rediscover yourself as a fresh being. But believe me, it is possible! You need to run certain filters based on your values and criteria so as to prioritise your growth. You have to become headstrong, embrace change and continue to evolve.

Something has to break from within before you outshine. Let go your past with acceptance of the divine patterns and your destiny. Living a life of 'ifs and buts' is just wasting some more coins of the limited stock of time you have been gifted. Excuse yourself of the mistakes you made due to your incapacity or inability to control fate. Excuse yourself for the mistakes made by your inexperience and your impatient self. Accept yourself as is!

> *'Wash yourself, of yourself.'*
> *– Rumi*

Rediscover!

Forgiveness – Become Unstoppable

Sometimes we hold on to bitter life experiences in the form of grudges against people who wronged us. We rent out that mental space free of charge! In fact, we bear its expenses by filling our life with negativity.

> *'Don't wait for people's apology to forgive them. Making them kneel down will only boost your ego. Forgiving them is your need not theirs. You have a long journey to travel, carrying a mental baggage will slow you down and you might give up. Free the space, FORGIVE UNCONDITIONALLY.'*

Forgiveness will never be easy on you. It will take a due course of time. Time gives perspective and strength to forgive. Give yourself time and space by distancing yourself from the people who harmed you, betrayed you, fooled you, used you, abused you. Often, it won't be possible to maintain the required distance, and they will keep repeating their behaviour each time you manage to clear yourself of their negativity. Create a space of your own where you can prevent their negativity from touching you. If you cannot physically create it, create one in your mind. A space that you can call your own, filled with compassion, warmth, love and positivity.

The most difficult thing in life after forgiving your own self is forgiving those on whom you had placed your complete trust. It is even harder to forgive your parents of all the fallacies they are capable of as human beings. You consider them your role model and a personification of all the ideals that you have been taught, which makes it difficult for you to perceive them as imperfect.

To heal completely, forgiveness is essential. Holding on is just that extra mental space that a forward-looking person cannot afford to lend for long. Think of all those failed relationships, all those criticisms and tactics used to show you down, all those childhood bruises that you have preserved, the times when your expectations were not taken care of, the times when your rights were not fulfilled, the times when you were helpless and could not fight back, all those grievances, all those past mistakes you keep on lamenting yourself for, the guilt that you have accumulated over the years.

Do you realise how heavy this load feels? Do you want to carry it for life? Pull out every single memory from your mind. While keeping the lesson, throw away all the bitterness associated with each one of them, one by one, purifying and bathing yourself in the light of positivity.

Forgiveness is the last and the hardest preparation that you need to do before you head on to find the treasures hidden within yourself. If you are finally able to practise forgiveness, you will progress on your journey of self-discovery by leaps and bounds until you become unstoppable!

Gratitude – Your Armour Against Negativity

If you do not flush out the past bitterness, it will take over you and turn into sadness and depression. Gratitude can serve as an armour to shield you from it. Gratitude is a sign of humility and servitude to God. When you thank God for both the good and bad things in your life, you acknowledge that power does not belong to you, but you derive it from the Higher Power. This mindset becomes the cornerstone of your successes in your life story. When you start considering your achievements as not just a result of your sole efforts but also a result of divine blessing, this mindset becomes the driving force bringing you out from situations of trials and losses, stopping you from falling into despair.

Gratitude reduces a multitude of toxic emotions, from envy and resentment to frustration and regret. Robert Emmons, a leading gratitude researcher, has conducted multiple studies on the link between gratitude and well-being. He reported that subjects who practise gratitude experience decreased anxiety and depression as well as demonstrate kinder behaviour towards others, express less aggression and have fewer physical complaints.

To attract positivity in your life, you have to be grateful to the Almighty for each and every experience of your past, good or bad. For example, if that man on the island had realised that if he had eaten the food that he was served, he could have got food poisoning, he would have had to spend more coins to pay for his treatment. Sometimes, the bad experiences in your life can be the best thing that can happen to you. When you retrace your journey backwards, it is only then that you realise that each and every piece of the jigsaw fits just at the place that it was meant to be.

> 'You can't connect the dots looking forward; you can only connect them looking backwards. So, you have to trust that the dots will somehow connect in your future. You have to trust in something — your gut, destiny, life, karma, whatever. This approach has never let me down, and it has made all the difference in my life.'
> – Steve Jobs

Many times, in our life, we experience so much pain, and we question 'why me?' We start comparing ourselves with others.

'How fortunate he is to be so happy-go-lucky. No worries at all. What a perfect life. Poor me! I wish I had one like this. Oh God! Have pity on me, please.'

We often find ourselves registering such complaints with our Creator in our hours of gloom. Not once do we realise that every smile we see has a behind-the-scenes story – 'unready' to be told. Each one of us has been given our own bucket of ease and hardships to carry, which is just the right weight and quantity for us to maintain a balance in life. The moment you start peeping into other people's buckets, chances are you might lose your balance and trip into ingratitude. The Almighty tests each person according to his strength and capacity of endurance. Nothing more, nothing less. What may feel heavy for you may feel light to the other and vice versa, because we all are unique creations of God. It is quite possible that a feather put on one person gives the same amount of pain and hurt as a rock put on another. The distribution is equitable, not equal.

Theory of Relativity

We live in a world of relativity. This implies that our brain understands and accepts things when it compares those with the rest. Our brain cannot comprehend the concept of absolute existence, and therefore, all our perceptions are subjective to our experiences. For example, we cannot understand pleasure without experiencing pain, or we cannot give meaning to light without experiencing darkness. But there are multiple shades of grey moving from black to white, each slightly lighter than the former. This is how our brain is designed to extract meaning. But if we use this brain function erroneously, it can lead us to discontentment and lack of peace. Let me tell you how.

Let's say you own one car. You are richer than those who own none, but less rich than a person who owns five cars. You can feel rich and poor at the same time, subjective to the frame of reference you are using to compare yourself. In your life, whenever you use a higher frame of reference, you will feel discontented of your possessions and ingratitude will creep in. Ingratitude fosters jealousy and competition.

The bad news is you will never be satisfied with what you have; instead, something inside will keep you craving for more and more. There is never an end to materialism, and hence this is an indefinite chase. You will always be restless, letting feelings of dissatisfaction and unhappiness build up. When you give attainment of material possessions a meaning of fulfilment, you deprive your soul of its food. Its food is peace, and no material thing can feed your immaterial soul with peace.

The good news is sometimes you need to have that pull in life. You need to feel dissatisfied, and you need to have the love for more and more so as to reach greater heights. But wisdom is to know where to feel that pull.

With respect to the material world, it is therefore advisable that you should keep a lower frame of reference in comparison to your possessions but a higher frame of reference with respect to intangibles like wisdom, intellect, good deeds, righteousness and so forth. Keeping a higher frame of reference with respect to these intangibles will no doubt leave you dissatisfied with your current state, but every time when you strive to chase the higher standard, you will transcend spiritually and feel a sense of fulfilment. Intangibles are the food that your soul craves in order to attain peace, but remember, absolute peace is unattainable in this world of relativity. Keep striving, your peace too is on a continuum.

It is particularly very difficult to thrive in an environment where everyone else is in a condition better than yours. No one likes to feel inferior. Passing through your trials without falling to compare yourselves with others is a big challenge. We are short-sighted and cannot unveil the future. Life is always changing and evolving. Nothing is permanent in this life. Hard times too shall pass. The friction that these challenges have rubbed you with will not leave you empty-handed. Allah will bless you in return with wisdom and insights, providing you the acceleration needed to gear up for brighter days.

There will be times when bad thoughts disempower you. You will feel low, and it is okay. Accept that you are human. Whenever a negative thought attacks you and your peace of mind, no matter where you are, empower yourself by reciting powerful words. In every day and every age, people know this secret. It is a brain thing! It's a method to harness your thoughts and divert it to positivity. You cannot stop thinking. It is not in your control, but you can harness your thoughts because thoughts create feelings, and feelings provoke you to do positive or negative behaviours. The most powerful things on this earth are words – positive or negative; they have the power to make things happen! May it then be a religious recital or a magic spell!

Whenever I find myself in such a state, I derive power from the beautiful names of Allah and in His name ask for protection from the negative thoughts. Whether it is rhythmic chanting on rosary beads or silently anchoring the positivity of those words on my fingers, my mind occupies itself in keeping count and getting mesmerised by its power. It gets distracted from the negativity that has been stewing within me.

Practise the Power of Gratitude

- Start your day with gratitude. Divide your life into different sections like health and well-being, spouse and children, family and friends, work and so forth. Thank God for all the blessings and ease that come your way in each of those areas.
- Make a gratitude jar. Whenever you are happy, write a note of what makes you feel so good. Keep filling the jar, and on days when you are feeling low, pick a note from the jar and read it.

Summary

- Let your past become a lesson and not a source of resentment and guilt.
- Let your memories, good or bad, become a source of power.
- Forgive others and, above all, your own self. Forgiveness is never easy; give yourself time and space to wipe off the negativity stored in your brain.
- Gratitude empowers you to lead a life of positivity and contentment.
- Keep away the bad thoughts by using the power of words.

Chapter Nine

Beyond Negative Space

There was a frog who was put in a pot of water at room temperature. The water was then put to heat, and the temperature slowly started rising. The frog remained comfortable as long as he could bear the heat and did not leave the pot. As he was so comfortable in his surroundings and lazy to explore and hop out of the pot, he continued to endure the rising temperature until he finally realised that he could not tolerate the environment anymore and should hop out, but unfortunately it was too late by then. The water had boiled hot enough to burn him alive.

Embracing Change – The Art of Letting Go

The story of the boiling frog is an excellent metaphor in many ways. People who are not futuristic and delay in embracing change are sometimes left very far behind. There are many examples of multinational brands that were not quick in embracing change and innovation, such as Kodak, Fuji, Panama, Nokia and so forth. Nokia, the pioneer in mobile communication of its time, missed this basic strategy and was overthrown by Apple. Nokia could neither rise to the changing technology nor upgrade itself in a timely manner, so much so that Samsung, an appliance manufacturer, became the next big giant after Apple. Nokia not only lost its market but was nowhere near the top.

Sometimes the uneasiness of jumping into the unknown from our cosy but stagnant spot blindsides us from the danger that we are about to hit. The skill of embracing the unknown and knowing the right time to do so is wisdom.

'As long as you are comfortable with the unknown, you remain alive.'

Digital Transformation demands that change management is carefully planned because people fear the transition. They resist change because they are afraid of the unknown. So, the change should not be pushed from the top; instead it should be co-authored with the people.

Now let's explore the need for change from a different perspective.

In this world of instant gratification where technology can serve you with just a single tap, self-control is the most difficult thing to do. The urge to react to a situation, the urge to get instant gains, the urge to get more and more leave us unsatisfied. Contentment is priceless while happiness can be bought. Buying a new car, decorating your house, having your favourite food, playing sports, hanging out with friends, going out for a movie are all small bits of happiness that you cherish but are often short-lived. They are food for your body, and as your body is impermanent so are these moments. The desire to make them permanent and everlasting is the mistake you often commit and, in that process, fall in the trap of your lustful desires. The lust for more and more keeps you restless, no matter how many riches you have collected. The balance lies in understanding the impermanence of this world and whatever is within it. It is necessary to understand that there is a cycle wherein there are periods of joy when life is in your favour, and there are periods of hardships when life challenges you so as to bring out the best in you. The biggest mistake you do is to try and alter this universal pattern.

> *'Life is a balance of holding on and letting go
> and wisdom is to know when to do what.'*
> *– Rumi*

Our brains operate on relativity, and that is how we value our life. For life to feel good, it has to feel bad too. Life in this world cannot be a constant but is a process of continuous change. Just imagine how boring your life will be if you have no challenges. The urge to hold on to things, people, places is a sign that you look forward to permanence. This might be the cry of your soul, but your body is destined to die. Embracing change is what gives flavour to life and makes it interesting. What would the world be like if it just had one season – let's say, spring would be the only season? Who would have valued the blooming flowers and the green scenery of nature when it is present all year round?

However, embracing change does not come easily, especially when it is hard to let go. Letting go the deceased, letting go your life with your parents and siblings when you start your own family, letting go your youth as you age, letting go your kids and giving them wings to fly out of your nest, letting go your habits, letting go your negative beliefs – everything is very hard to let go until finally, you let go your body and transition into the world of permanence, your final abode. Many people hide behind the limiting belief that a person can only change while he is young. Always remember, you are never too old to change. It is your intention and will, that bring about the change and they are ageless.

Living Like a Vagabond

If I go back in time, my grandparents had migrated from India at the time of partition and settled in Karachi. I had opened my eyes in the city near the Arabian coast. Karachi, being a metropolitan city, had the best colleges and universities the country had to offer. Hence, I did not get a chance to move out of the city or to live in a hostel seeking education or employment. Neither our ancestral homes were in the country to which we could plan a trip and explore the countryside. Therefore, the city became my entire universe until I got married and relocated to the Middle East with my spouse.

It was here that I realised the horizon was much wider than I had thought. I happened to meet people from different places of Pakistan who had settled in the Middle East as well as people from other countries of the world – people of different colour, languages, lifestyle and values; it was an opportunity I never got living back home.

To settle in a different part of the world with a sense of not belonging to the land we chose to live in was a challenging decision. Living in fully furnished apartments where our possessions were limited, we literally used to pack our suitcases and move to a new house in just a single day. We shifted three houses in a period of four years and then went to Dubai, leaving Bahrain, the country where I had birthed two of my children, a place I had so many memories associated with.

For a person who had lived in one place for almost 25 years of her life and then moved from one place to another in just a span of eight years, this was super challenging and completely out of her comfort zone. I am someone who would emotionally attach myself with people, places, things and who never learnt to let go of my possessions. I still remember holding on to my favourite books, the gifts I had received since my early childhood, not even throwing the gift wrapper. I tried doing the same for my children, the artworks from their preschool, their toys, their clothes, but moving continuously did not allow me the luxury to hoard these possessions. Letting them go was the most difficult thing to do, but practice made me good at it.

The first time I had to do this, it was emotionally devastating, but then I started feeling lighter and lighter. Associations are good but should be coupled with periods of detachments so as to foster new energies. Sometimes you associate emotions with things without realising that they trap your energies and burden your soul. Physical dissociation is followed by emotional dissociation – letting go of the burden of your past, learning to let go your old self, your old ways, your old beliefs, your old habits that no longer serve you and limit you from looking beyond the horizon. You learn to live a carefree life, the life of a vagabond.

Building Resilience – Your Flexible and Adaptive Muscle
The moment you accept the pattern of change, you learn resilience because you have stopped holding on and learnt to thrive, no matter what challenges you face when you are out of your comfort zone.

'Resilience is the ability to come out from a challenging negative situation with greater wisdom and more groomed and developed self.

You are truly resilient if you can look beyond the surface to the depths of those unfavourable experiences, extracting greater meaning signalling you to dive deeper into yourself so as to unlock your potential for change and growth thereby fulfilling your life purpose.'

Resilience is the opposite of a victim mindset. A victim mindset is one where you are not in control of anything; everything outside you controls you – whether it's bad weather, lack of opportunities, absence of physical or emotional support, low finances, an irritating neighbour, a nasty cat, the government, the irregular system, the conspiracies and plots against you. You name it and it will become the reason for you not to break through your share of challenges. It is an easy and lazy way to not get in control of yourself and blame the third party for your downfall.

Resilience teaches you to create opportunities amidst all the challenges and hardships, instead of waiting for things happen to you. If you are unemployed or fired from your job, and despite a good amount of job searching and recruitment agency leads you are unable to get a job, it means there is an underlying opportunity behind closed doors. Maybe Allah is signalling you through these challenges to be an entrepreneur, to build your own door and create opportunities for yourself. Self-doubting your talent or lamenting upon the job market will only land you into self-victimisation. But in order for you to build a door, it is necessary for you to accept this change. Not only this, you also need to be tough to the call, rise to the crisis and learn to swim in strong currents. Flexibility is a key skill to adapt and thrive in abrupt situations.

Solution-Focused Approach

Exercise your mind to focus on the possibilities and opportunities that can be created rather than focusing on the problems. Yes, it is foolish to hide from the bitter realities, but living with them, letting your problems nag you and, not taking action for the better is stupidity and waste of energy. Polish your problem-solving skills and take action. Believe in the goodness of your actions and be optimistic about the results. Don't shy away from changing your course of action if you realise your mistake. Let your ego not come in your way of accepting your fault.

Consistency – The Secret Behind Persistence

Imagine you came up with an innovative plan. You spontaneously took the decision to take action. You are on fire. You invest all your energy and time. You lose the balance in your life. Everything in your life comes to a standstill. You compromise your time with your family and friends; your daily chores are pushed to the side because this fantastic plan of yours is in action. All your efforts and energy are focused on this project, and then after a few days, all of a sudden, your energy dies. From peak performance, you reach the lowest of the low. The motivation bubble bursts, and your master plan stops abruptly in the middle of nowhere. Have you ever experienced such a situation? What could have gone wrong? Are your projects always left hanging in the middle?

When you spontaneously take an action, you push yourself too hard. The analogy is similar to that of a sprint race and a marathon. If you are working on a small project with shorter timelines, this approach is helpful, but for projects with longer timelines, bottlenecks and external dependence, this approach will not sustain you for long. You will get tired before you reach the finish line. You will be overwhelmed by the amount of work; as time passes, you will be set back by self-doubt, and it is highly likely that you will give up.

It is better to take small consistent steps towards your goal than to take big leaps. This will make you persistent in your efforts, and each and every goal of yours will reach completion.

Growth Mindset – Accelerate Your Learning Curve

Nothing can be more devastating to your growth than the mantra of 'my way or the highway'. This egoistic approach of doing things just your way kills learning. You need to keep your ego at the side in order to learn.

Meet new people from different backgrounds, different age groups and different cultures so that you widen your perception. For a long time, it was taboo to marry people outside your culture or ethnic background, but in reality, intercultural marriages are a great opportunity for personal and generational growth where both partners come together, learning new ways and perspectives of looking at things and solving problems. When you remain stuck in the same environment with similar ways of living life, you are as good as dead.

Because your points of view are very restricted to the small group to which you belong – perhaps your style of parenting, your general outlook towards life, the different definitions of important life concepts like success, purpose, fulfilment – their meanings are also limited. You are unable to widen your horizon. Hence, the truth for you is the only one perspective you know since birth; it is the basis on which you form your reality and base your judgements. From this truth sprouts racism, sects, intolerance and self-righteousness, because there is no opportunity for people from different backgrounds to come together and discuss their realities and perspectives.

> *'Tolerance is to understand someone's point of view without the need to accept it.'*

No single human or a single society has absolute intelligence. We all have bits and pieces of knowledge that we acquire through observation, experience and social learning. This formulates collective intelligence, and these multiple intelligences when combined together form the masterminds and the rich knowledge base that has been the basis of human evolution since times unknown. To accelerate the process of evolution of human intelligence, Allah sent Prophets, revealing to them the divine wisdom.

> *'Divine wisdom is the superset while human wisdom is its subset.'*

In fact, Allah has divided us into tribes Himself, having different mindsets and values and ways of doing things. Have you questioned the reason behind such a diverse distribution? Human survival is not possible if all people have the same perspectives, same learning and same cognitions. Not everyone is supposed to have the same experiences.

> *'Globalisation is convenient, but diversity is evolutionary.'*

People have migrated since their inception in search of a better climate and better resources. Would human sustenance be possible if they were to be stagnant in one place?

Artificial Intelligence (AI) works on a similar principle of a rich knowledge base by which robots learn different behaviours. Scientists collect all possible perceptions and ways in which a human response is generated in a particular situation and feed this collective intelligence to programme a robot. Robots learn different behaviours through this collective intelligence.

Learning never stops and is not limited to any age or time. Learning directly impacts our brain as we build neural connections and networks, which leads to crystallised intelligence. You become a valuable resource and a beneficial asset in this world by contributing your wisdom and intellect in bringing ease to people's lives.

Dive Deeper into Your Inner Self

Connect yourself with the absolute source of knowledge because relative knowledge is always biased, a result of social conditioning based on limited experiences of a group, society or culture.

The challenge is how will you identify which source is divine and which one is relative? Contemplation and reflection on your life within and without give you the opportunity to explore the deeper secrets of this universe and helps you find the true purpose of your existence. Reflecting upon the universe, spending time in nature, grounding and connecting yourself with Earth from which you are created will not only refresh your energy but will also gift you some very powerful insights.

Follow your intuition. Human intuition (inspired through soul) and reasoning/intellect(mind) are two gifts that – if used intelligently – can lead to the excellence of human existence in this world and beyond.

'There is a magic in every soul. Discover the magic in your soul. Infuse it with the heavenly fragrance (divine wisdom) that diffuses near and far.'

- Do something unique. Embrace your individuality. Take the road less travelled.
- Travel the world. Don't be stagnant, keep exploring
- Take long walks in nature. Do gardening. Breathe in fresh air. Practise yoga.

Circle of Positivity

You may have noticed when certain people enter a room, the atmosphere suddenly changes. Their presence is soulful; it lights up every face, and there is an air of positivity around. If you know someone like this, keep him for good.

People carry energies, and people with good vibes uplift you. Build your inner circle with positive-minded people. You are likely the average of the five people you surround yourself with. Inspire yourself by people who have been through similar journeys and have come out successful. It will give you the strength to move through darker times with hope and optimism.

Positive people have solutions to all problems, while negative people have problems with every solution. This does not mean that you have to completely cut ties with people whom you do not get along with much. Every experience is a learning, and so is this. While it is necessary to know what 'to do' in life, at the same time it is essential to know ***what not to do or become***. Such people are very good examples to teach you this very important lesson. Sometimes these people can be a family member, your blood relation. In an attempt to avoid toxicity, you break ties, which is an extreme reaction. Maintain enough distance so that they do not suck your energy, but completely severing ties is not recommended for your learning to be full circle. Instead of holding grudges and absorbing their negativity, thank all those negative people in your life that made you who you are today.

Build a Healthy Lifestyle

It is said you are what you eat.

> *'Tell me what you eat, and I will tell you what you are.'*
> *– Anthelme Brillat-Savarin*

Build a healthy eating habit, making sure that you have your greens and avoid starchy and sugary foods that can make you lazy. A sedentary lifestyle is also very harmful, especially in today's world where there is hardly any physical activity. Work on including fitness and physical exercises as a part of your routine.

All successful people have one thing in common. They follow an early morning ritual so that they start their day with positive energy. Make sure you are an early riser. If you work on your physiology, it will automatically elevate your mood and keep you away from the negative space.

Summary

- Learn to let go. Embrace change.
- Believe in the impermanence of things, and it will help you to let go easily.
- Surround yourself with positivity, with a circle of people who uplift one another. Also work on an active and healthy lifestyle. Your physical fitness will lead to your emotional fitness.
- Engage yourself in continuous learning and explore your inner world. Take up new challenges and be open to adventures.

Chapter Ten

The Science of the Seen and the Signs of the Unseen

Seeing Is Confirming
It is said that 'seeing is believing', but I strongly disagree. Belief is supposed to be unseen. Anything that our five senses can endorse is never a belief. This means that 'seeing is confirming'.

On the contrary, science revolves around the 'seen'. Anything that can be proven by our senses is conveniently termed as genuine. Would you use a white bedsheet or a relatively darker shade? Why? Would you prefer to sit on a carpet or a floor? Why?

I remember sometime back I was prone to asthma. The doctor asked me to take measures to avoid dust as much as I could. Meanwhile, a salesperson came at our doorstep to give a demo of a very hi-tech steamer that would make every inch of the house sparkly clean. And surely it did. The equipment was amazing. It could take out dust and filth from places we had assumed to be really clean. She gave a demo to extract dust out of the mattress my little girl used to sleep on every night. The sales lady asked, 'Would you allow your child to sleep while inhaling dust particles this close to her nose?' 'No way! Her mattress is clean,' I said defensively. Then the monster machine did its work, and it was unbelievable how much dust came out of just a patch of the mattress. This made me wonder how much do humans rely on their power to see. As long as we can't see it, it is acceptable; the moment we saw it, it became useless. I used to use coloured and printed bedsheets, which would conveniently stay on my bed for days. Suddenly it occurred to me that I should try using white sheets, which I generally avoided again because they get dirty easily. When I spread the white sheet, I couldn't keep it for more than two days, and I would make sure that our feet were super clean before we dared sit. The kids were strictly asked to wash their feet before jumping on the super clean white sheets. The sheets get equally get dirty – whether white or coloured. It's just that it's more visible on white. This made me question: If we cannot see something, does it really mean it does not exist? From that day on, I preferred offering prayers on a clean, wiped floor instead of a prayer mat! The feeling of prostrating directly on the ground has not only made me humble but also gave me a sense of freshness and purity instead of prostrating on a colourful cloth with design patterns that stimulated my brain and distracted my attention from prayer. My point in sharing these experiences with you is to emphasise how much our reliance is on the 'seen'.

The Science of the Seen – All That Glitters Is Not Gold

All inventions and theories are based on our power to see, in short, our five senses, which dangerously implies that anything that our five senses cannot prove apparently does not exist! This is not to undermine the technological advancements made through scientific discoveries. In fact, the science of the seen leads to the signs of the unseen, and both work in parallel for us to contemplate and discover the secrets of this Universe – seen and unseen. Scientifically speaking, all our senses are connected to our brain, whether it is our vision, hearing or sensation. All signals go to the brain, which in turn generates a response.

Have you ever realised how easily humans can be fooled if they only rely on their five senses?

The fact that humans primarily rely on their five senses is much more exploited as in the case of the electronic media. A dumb machine would broadcast information 24/7 to feed your brain whatever it would like you to watch and hear. We affirm at once to it because we can actually see and hear it. In this way, human minds are controlled on a mass scale.

Businesses play around with the human mind. Before launching a product, they work more on human psychology than on the product itself. Beauty naturally appeals to humans. You would have noticed how the branding and packaging of a product play the most important role in its sales.

Once I was at the supermarket grocery shopping. As I was looking at apples, I noticed there were some apples that outshone the others, being more attractive to the eyes. As a customer, naturally my hand would reach the ones that were more visually pleasing presuming that they might be juicier than the others. For a moment, I held back my instinct and started examining the ones that were not shiny. I noticed that they were fresher and firmer than their shinier counterparts, which on careful examination turned out to have turned wrinkles and marks. Sometimes the mark was hidden under the supplier's sticker. The apples that were visually more attractive were the old and defective pieces, waxed and polished so as to hide their defects. The unpolished apples were not tempting at first glance but were, in fact, the freshest in that batch.

Many times, what you see is not what is real. For instance, you may see photos especially on Facebook or Instagram, and you start assuming how happy and contented other people's lives appear to be. This may sometimes create desires, leaving you dissatisfied with your own life. It may come as a shock to you when you actually get to know their inside stories. Research led by Melissa Hunt, a psychology professor at the University of Pennsylvania, reveals that there is a causal link between time spent on social media and depression and loneliness.

Belief – The Fundamental Brain Code

As discussed earlier, belief is a set of code on which the brain operates. Depending on the code, the brain formulates its reality, and that reality is subjective to life experiences, cognitions and social conditioning. It is very important that the code that is written serves for the benefit of the individual in a holistic sense; that is, it should serve for the benefit of mind, body and soul and create a balance. There shouldn't be collateral damage in serving any of the three. However, understanding which beliefs to adopt and which ones to let go – acquired as a result of social learning – is not an easy task. For example, you believe that every time it rains, some misfortune will happen. This belief will make sure that whenever it rains, you are overtaken by the emotion of fear, the fear of misfortune. Fear will manifest itself in your cowardly attitude. If you are driving, your hands will tremble, you will lose focus, and you will likely manifest the reality of an accident. If you are about to close a deal in a sales meeting, you will likely lose your confidence, which would be visible enough for the customer to not trust you. A belief as minor as this can create a reality where your actions will be in complete obedience to this superstition. You self-fulfil the prophecy.

Beliefs can also serve as justifications to your setbacks – sometimes positively and sometimes negatively. A person who believes in destiny can utilise this belief both ways. If he puts his 100 percent effort and is still unable to achieve the desired result, his belief in destiny can de-stress him from the pressure of unachieved success; whereas if the same person does not put any effort with the belief that if it is destined to happen it will, it will limit him from trying, and he will blame destiny for not giving him opportunities.

Some self-limiting beliefs are

- I am too old to change myself.
- There is no hope in the future of this country.
- If you will rise against oppression your voice will be suppressed.
- What change can a single person bring; the system will never change.
- People will not accept me the way I am.
- I am not good enough.
- It is extremely bad not to help people.

These beliefs are formed as a result of a few instances that then turn into generalisations. These instances become the evidence converting these beliefs into proven facts. People at an individual level or as a nation start believing these notions and define their reality accordingly. Conspiracy theories land people into self-victimisation. They are not able to take responsibility for their condition. Therefore, it is very important to feed your brain with healthy beliefs that are utilised in a way that serve you the most and do not harm or limit you in any way.

Can humans survive without a belief system? Let me create an analogy of the human brain with the CPU of a computer as it is an invention inspired by the human brain. Can a computer system – which includes the CPU and BIOS – function without an operating system? The system will not operate, just like the human being. For example, an atheist who does not believe in God believes in something else, that is, the non-existence of God. Just because he does not believe in God's master plan does not mean he does not believe. He believes in cause and effect and things happening by chance. This shows that belief is the fundamental building block of the human brain.

Often people utterly disagree with others who hold beliefs that contradict theirs. If you want to make someone your enemy, mock and ridicule his beliefs! This is one of the main reasons for animosity and war amongst people. If you wish better for someone and do not want him to be captured by his self-limiting belief, think of better ways to convince him to upgrade his beliefs, provided you do not blindly follow yours. And if you yourself are a blind follower, you should first work on convincing yourself as to why you believe in something. Or else you will fall prey to 'confirmation bias', a term in psychology where one has the tendency to search for, interpret, favour and recall information in a way that confirms his or her pre-existing beliefs. Moreover, make sure your belief is just not the first thing that you heard or was taught by your parents or society. It is human nature that the first thing you come across becomes your frame of reference.

Looking at this from another angle, it is, for this reason, very important to create good first impressions because people are most likely going to judge you on the basis of the frame of reference you set in the first meeting.

This gives rise to the question, how do you identify whether you hold healthy beliefs, and what are the parameters for measuring the authenticity of a divine belief? Divine beliefs cannot be proven by our five senses; relying on physical senses to prove them is not a good choice either, as we have already discussed how human senses can be exploited to fool you. Heaven, hell, angels, the afterlife and even God are all unseen, and there is no empirical evidence to support them. Does this mean they are not true? Divine beliefs can be verified through signs and not through empirical evidences. The witness is the inner eye.

The Inner Eye – Your Spiritual Heart

Do you know that your heart can see? The sense of this feeling is not the same as the physical sense of see, hear, touch or smell; but it is the inner sight, the inner vision.

Apart from your five senses, you have the heart that is your inner eye and the spiritual centre. It is coded with a divine code called your natural disposition, which is the frame of reference to judge yourself on the moral scale. Natural disposition is pure and knows how to discriminate right from wrong. The human capability that distinguishes you from other creations is your power to choose and judge. Your natural disposition guides you to make good choices and take right decisions. However, it is overridden by environmental conditioning at a very young age, and the morals of your environment become your relative morals. Your beliefs, values and ideals then are relative to the time you live in and the people you surround yourself with. This is why company matters.

Your spiritual heart can be imagined as a crystal glass that shines and sparkles but loses its lustre and gets tinted when it is burdened by deeds that go against the manufacturer's code – that is, your natural disposition. Just like if a car is mishandled, the engine becomes weak, so does the human being. You are overcome by guilt and stress of going against your primary code. As this burden grows, it gets heavier and starts manifesting in your physical body in the form of illnesses and in your mind in the form of psychological issues of stress, anxiety and depression. This is not to say that your physical illnesses or psychological states are caused by the unrest inside, but they strongly correlate to the kind of energies you hold and your state of mind. People with negative emotions like guilt, shame, resentment and regret are more likely to get autoimmune disorders than people whose minds are free from anxiety and stress.

Going against your natural disposition ruins your inner and outer peace and you exist in a state of continuous conflict with yourself.

Natural Disposition – The Natural Code
The Natural Code is the code that is part of your spiritual identity just like genes are part of your physical body. It is the basis of your natural

disposition. It is the manufacturer's code – absolute, read-only, unchanged that resides in your spiritual heart. This natural code is responsible for maintaining the balance of mind, body and soul.

Social Conditioning – The Cognitive Code

A belief that has roots in our upbringing, environment and social learning accompanied by our own perceptions of those experiences formulates the first category, which I call the Cognitive Code. This code is relative and can be edited and upgraded as a person's intellect or experience grows. Cognitive code resides in your mind. It is subjective and can be your religious, cultural and societal beliefs and ideals, the values taught by your parents and teachers and so forth.

The closer your cognitive code is to your natural code, the more efficiently you will operate in this world and the closer you will be to inner peace. The lesser it is, the farther you will be from inner peace and contentment.

When your actions clash with your cognitive code, you are in a state of conflict. In order to get rid of guilt, you either need to upgrade your cognitive code or make sure your actions conform to it. In psychology, this is called cognitive dissonance. There will be times when you will engage in rituals, social behaviours and daily interactions in order to conform to your cognitive code, but you will feel a sense of emptiness inside. You will be part of festivals, religious rituals and cultural norms that make no sense to you, but you will follow them unquestionably. You will feel emptiness and restlessness inside, depriving you of balance and peace, and then your spiritual heart will guide you to upgrade your cognitive code to align as close as possible to your natural code. However, for this to happen, you must reach a state of spiritual awakening where you can look beyond your five senses and decipher the mystery of the unknowns.

Then there will be times when your actions will not conform to the cognitive code, which is already in alignment with your natural code. Your desires may overpower you, and you may breach the standards that you have set for yourself to follow. You may feel a sense of guilt because you're not in alignment with either of your codes. You will try to somehow fix the cognitive code because it can be changed, so you can distance yourself from the guilt that's bugging you. Often, you will be successful in suppressing the voice of your spiritual heart and your conscience, which is there to guide you, and it will quieten down. Your life will reach a state of unbalance wherein there is no inner or outer peace. For example, what do you think goes on in the mind of a murderer or a thief? How does he overcome the feelings of guilt inside him? He keeps on justifying his actions and gives self-serving excuses to his actions. This is when your spiritual heart has lost so much of its lustre that it stops guiding you and you lose your moral compass.

Ideally, the cognitive code should match the natural code, but we do not exist in a perfect world. From time to time, you will be overpowered by your inner desires and temptations and will deviate from your natural code, but as long as you repent and restart your efforts, you will be in control of yourself.

The Signs of the Unseen – Follow Your Heart

There is a strong link between the world of 'seen' and the world of 'unseen'. Just as seen is authenticated by our five senses, the unseen is authenticated by the signs. The signs of the unseen can only be witnessed through the science of the seen. You use your five senses to perceive the science of the seen in order to unveil the signs of the unseen. The lightning, the rain, the sun, the moon, all are signs of the Unseen – that is, the Creator Allah knows our reliance on our five senses and hence he has shown us these signs to believe in the unseen because the presence of unseen can only be seen through these signs. These signs are codes and can only be deciphered by the ones who follow their heart. What tools do you need in order to decode these signs?

Peace – Your Ultimate Destination

I relate peace with this situation that I often come across while driving on the road. There are cameras placed at very short distances to keep a check on over-speeding. The best bet to avoid speed tickets is to obediently follow the speed limits by setting the cruise control and be at peace. But there will be times when you are over-speeding because of an emergency, when you are in a rush or are not paying attention, and this is when your peace will be disrupted. You will keep on checking the speedometer. Thus, achieving perfect and absolute peace while we are a part of this world is simply wishful thinking.

You can only RIP (Rest in Peace) once you transition from this world into the next and experience death. Till then, let us all wish and greet each other with the peace that we all desperately seek. I wish you peace and blessings of your Creator in this world. May you get as close to it as possible before you experience the ultimate peace.

The Spiritual Awakening – Deciphering Your Natural Code

How will you know what speed limit you are supposed to follow? In other words, how will you decipher your natural code in order to follow it? The only code that you have understood all your life is the one taught to you by your teachers, parents and peers in the form of the religion you are born into, the culture you are raised in and the social groups you are part of.

There will come a time in your life when you will reach spiritual awakening, a time when you will question your beliefs and values. You will question the religion that you are born into and the cultural norms that you often give in to.

This is the time when your spiritual heart is enlightened, and you begin to witness the signs of the unseen and can crack your natural code.

- **Reflection and contemplation: Strengthen your intuition**
  Look beyond the surface; try to read between the lines. The heart, intuition, contemplation and reflections of the universe give insights into the world of unseen.
- **Meditation: Detox your mind**
  You need to purify your mind by acquiring divine knowledge. It is the food for your soul. Also, purify from negative thoughts through meditation. Unfortunately, thoughts are beyond your control. Negative thoughts can overpower you if you entertain them. They are like clouds that pass through the sky. Let them pass over you without internalizing them to be true.
- **Fast: Detox your body**
  Purify your body by eating pure and healthy food.
- **Spiritual retreat: Detox your soul**
  Spiritually cleanse jealousy, anger, resentment, regret, expectations and desires, all of which are toxic for your soul.
- **Cleanliness is next to godliness**
  Clean your outer body and keep yourself and your outfits pure.
- **Mute the social noise**
  In order for you crack your natural code and experience your soul's revival, you have to mute the social noise.

Summary

- When logic ends, faith begins! You take a shift from the world of seen to the world of unseen. Intuition takes precedence over the five senses.

- In order to take a leap of faith, you need to listen to your spiritual heart.
- It is very important to analyse your beliefs and their outcomes. Check the ones that serve you and get rid of the ones that limit you.
- The closer your social conditioning is to your natural disposition, the more you will be closer to peace.
- Absolute peace does not exist in this temporary world.

Chapter Eleven

The Secret to Abundance

Barakah – The Unseen Abundance

When you invest your money in a bank, you see your savings grow tangibly. Every quarter or at the end of the year, your balance sheet is the evidence of your money that has multiplied over time. This logically implies that your net total increases with visible financial growth. But what if I told you that there is something more powerful with a greater ROI – something that is beyond any logical explanation, from the world of unseen, a blessing from the Supreme Power. It is called *'Barakah'*, which is Arabic for 'blessing'.

Barakah is a difficult concept whose existence cannot be proved empirically, but the inner eye can see its fruits and feel the pleasure of this abundance. There are signs that can make its presence felt. I understood this when I started cultivating my kitchen garden. Being a nature lover, I used to spend a lot of time in the mud, ploughing the soil and feeling the earth. I enjoy grounding myself. Connecting with earth always gives me a feeling of peace. It balances my energies, and I feel all the negative energy leaving my body. I sowed the land with different vegetable seeds – tomatoes, chillies, coriander, onions, potatoes – saved from the waste I collected while cooking food. Peels and skins made good compost, enriching the soil while the seeds were like long-term investments buried underneath the soil. I kept on watering the soil, in the hope of getting good returns. In a few months, I got a return, an ROI that nobody could have given me. With a single seed, I now had plenty of succulent red tomatoes hanging down a very delicate branch.

This made me understand the concept of abundance that comes directly from the unseen. And from that day I started sowing seeds: seeds of my time, my money, my skills, my knowledge, giving them to the Unseen, anything and everything in which I wished abundance. This is the secret to abundance in this life, an abundance whose outcome cannot be measured by any instrument that has ever been calibrated or calculated by any formula that mathematics can ever formulate.

The Psyche Behind Hoarding

My grandparents migrated from India, leaving behind their property and land, choosing a life of hardship over the luxuries that they were so used to. They had borne all this to give us a better future, and I am very grateful for their sacrifices. They literally started their lives all over again in Pakistan, saving bit by bit to build a shelter that we could call home. Migration is never easy, leaving your attachments and associations behind for a greater cause. Somewhere in the middle of providing us security and comforts, they had lost themselves. These were people who owned orchards and farms and had a dozen workers always ready to serve them. Suddenly they were in a place where they had two suitcases in hand, small children in their laps and a temporary shelter that could barely withstand harsh weather. The stories of their migration move me from within. I remember one of their experiences when very heavy rainfall resulted in their belongings drifting through the rainwater in the streets.

A sudden and drastic change in your life where you have left behind the life you've known, loss of association, can create within you a vacuum. As this vacuum increases, it gradually starts sucking both your material and intangible possessions inside it, trying to fill that empty space. You start holding on to them very tightly in fear of not losing them ever again.

Learning from my environment, hoarding became second nature to me. I would hoard clothes, shoes, bags, books, all kinds of junk and would get emotionally disturbed if ever I had to let go any of them. Many people in my household had a similar personality; we kept criticising each other for not letting go but, when it came to them, they were bigger hoarders than the others.

The Art of Giving

Hoarders are not misers. They may do a lot of charity, but they find it easier to buy something and give it to others rather than give things from their possessions. However, hoarding comes with a cost. It's a burden that your soul carries, and you don't realise until it starts spilling. It is a heavy emotional baggage that you associate with things, and this trapped up energy takes its toll. So that you are not trapped in this cycle, you should 'give' from the things that you love the most. Randomly give your favourite pen to your friend as a gesture of your friendship; give your clothes or accessories to the needy, prioritizing your close relatives. When you watch those close to you benefitting from your giveaways, your heart will expand more and you will be encouraged to let go even more.

Remember the story of the siblings who fought over a toy. Teach your children to give by being a role model yourself. Build a long-term positive intention to give – not to give as any kind of bargain with each other but teach them to have the intention of giving their beloved things to the Unseen so that they are multiplied.

You might think that when you will have enough wealth or provision then you will give, but the secret to abundance does not work this way. It is a leap of faith and a test of the Unseen and of your trust in Him, when you do not have enough but you believe in the power of giving Him. Thus, in order to attract abundance in your life, you need to spend from your current provisions, no matter how less they are. Even if it sounds very illogical, it is backed by the history of this world. No one has ever become poor by giving.

Therefore, when it comes to what you want in life – whether money, fame, recognition, respect – when you spend from what is on your plate, you will certainly attract more of it, so much so that a time will come when your cup overflows

زكاة *(Zakah)* is an Arabic word which means to grow, purify and increase, and the Islamic ritual of sharing a small percentage of your wealth with the poor and needy is in fact a way to purify and attract abundance in life.

Uplifting each other leads to the dynamic growth of society at large. It builds a strong support system and healthy society. When people uplift each other, it reduces the negative emotions of not only the taker but also the giver.

By empowering others, you experience inner peace and contentment, a sense of fulfilment and satisfaction, which is a remedy for depression and anxiety. You unconsciously lessen your own burdens by healing people in distress or misfortune. Giving from your provisions releases your emotional baggage attached to material things. Your possessions do not own you anymore; you start owning them and decide where and when to use them. You have better opportunities to utilise them, by alleviating the pain of others, thereby bringing ease into your own life. This eventually leads to your freedom from materialism.

A person who might seem self-centred to you must be helping people in ways you may not have an idea about. It is often the material and financial side of help that is mostly noticeable, but people can be uplifted in many ways. One of them can be financial support, but people help others based on what personal and unique strengths they possess. Some may be gifted with intelligence, some with compassion, others with influence. They utilise these gifts in empowering others. Therefore, gossiping about others will only do harm to you because they will be enjoying the fruits of abundance while you will be counting their flaws. The fact is, what you only perceive as a form of giving is that which is valuable to you and difficult for you to let go or you yourself are short of. If you consider wealth as valuable, you will regard wealth as the supreme form of giving. If you are short of emotional support, you will value it as the highest form of support.

An unemployed person will be in a very different emotional state from that of a person who is good at his finances. A negative emotional state will hinder him to take bold and calculated actions. He will be overpowered by the fear of misery. Usually when people are caught up in a financial crisis, they lose hope and are low on emotional resources. Boosting their motivation, giving them good counsel and validating their strengths help build their self-esteem and give them hope to keep going until they hit their provision pot. This is also a form of giving.

You must be wondering what the provision pot is. It is not a potluck or jackpot but instead a pot of blessings that belongs to you. The provisions can include food, wealth, respect, recognition, fame and so forth. The presupposition that your provision is pre-defined and you need to put efforts to get it keeps you firm in taking action, while at the same time you are patient enough to wait for the results of your efforts, which in some cases may require extra time.

Consider this situation. You are in a close relationship with someone with whom you don't get along well. Being in their presence is so toxic that it burns you from inside out. The grudge that is between you and him takes up your mental space and disrupts your peace. Do you know what is the best way to convert this negative emotion into a gush of positive energy that illuminates your entire existence? Support him when he needs help. You must be wondering whether I am talking sense! But the fact of the matter is empowering someone you have a grudge against, empowers you to heights beyond your imagination. Help him not for his sake but your own. It is a manifestation of your forgiveness for him. There is no doubt that forgiveness elevates your status and helps you reach heights that you could not earlier because of your negativity towards him that was blocking your way. Your mental space is precious, use it wisely!

One thing that is very important is to make sure that you help people to help themselves. Always remember you cannot help someone who does not want to help himself. You should not make people dependent upon your support and service to them. Because, in that case, you will be spoiling them and teaching them to abuse you whenever they are lazy to put in their own efforts.

Consider this situation. You have a brother who is low on finances and depends on your support to run his expenses. If you do not empower him and instead pamper him because he's your younger brother by bearing his expenses, you will ruin his motivation to earn his own living. Chances are that he would always look for your support and would never be able to stand on his own feet. Actions are relevant in their context, and you cannot implement them disregarding the time and space they had been taken. It is likely that your mother had asked you to be helping and caring towards your younger brother, the kind of care that you had provided when he was small and dependent would not be the same and as frequent even when he has grown up. The problem arises when you keep believing that he still needs the same support. If you truly care for him, you should teach him independence and not reliance.

Therefore, it is very important to build healthy boundaries, which include financial boundaries as well. This will ensure that people are empowered, and you maintain a healthy relationship with them without compromising your own self.

Some people hesitate in taking support from others. There can be many reasons for such an attitude. They may not want to take favours from others because they don't want to cause any kind of inconvenience or they fear that they would have to compensate them equally or they consider themselves self-sufficient or they don't want to give credit to others for their support and want to do everything by themselves. Whatever may be the reason, it limits them to build a relationship of care.

There is this excellent Prophetic tradition called '*iyadah*' – that is, visiting the sick, which promotes an attitude of care and compassion for others. However, if you follow rituals without being taught the essence, the soul gets lost with the departure of the sages of those times. Without foundations to stand on, society cannot incorporate these traditions in their changing culture and lifestyle, and these beautiful traditions go into oblivion.

Until recently, people did follow this tradition but in a way that made it more of an inconvenience than an ease. People gathered at the sick person's house, making it into a kind of family gathering, having conversations with each other. Those who did not show up would be criticised. Is that what this tradition was meant for? It was not meant for a social gathering; it was meant as relief for the sick and not to overburden his family with undue hospitality or to humiliate others for not paying a visit. Since the tradition did not carry the essence and soul, with our evolving and fast lifestyles it has stopped making sense.

Recently, I fell sick. My neighbour messaged me to ask if she could cook food for me. I am the type who never asks for any favour or help from another person, but this time was different. I said yes.

Why should I deprive her of earning so many *'ḥasanāt'* (blessings or rewards) just because I would be obliged to return her the favour? And in the first place, who am I to return her the favour. It's never between me and her. It's between her and Allah, and who else would be the best to reward her than Him.

These small acts draw people closer. I got the chance to try some nice Palestinian food. I felt the warmth and care of a neighbour, which by spending some bucks I could never have.

We pressurise our relationships to follow a give-and-take attitude. We are not building relationships, we are doing business.

'We have already invited them, now it is their turn!'
'We gave them that gift, see what they got us!'
'If someone sends you food, don't send empty pots.'

I had a very nice experience at the party of one of my Romanian friends. Romanians have the tradition of opening gifts randomly without seeing who gave what. Since I belonged to subcontinent where even wedding gifts/envelopes – *'neeyota'* – are marked and noted in a register, I was surprised to see a Sunnah being followed in such a nice manner. Romanians say that gifts are for sharing happiness and not weighing each other on materialistic scales.

Later, I jokingly said to my husband that had this been implemented in our society, everyone would turn up with the cheapest gift available. Because nobody would know who gave the gift!

Who are we humans to reward each other or return favours? Do you know what is the missing link in our relationships, the link that connects human relationships? The link is God. Doing things *'Fee SabeelAllah' (in the path of Allah)*. By the way, for me it was the most valuable *Sadaqah* (charity) that my friends and neighbours did . As I am writing this, it seems odd because we are not used to these terms. We think *Sadaqah* is just for the poor. We have been conditioned to think that if someone does anything for you as *Sadaqah* or for Allah's sake, it is something humiliating or not of value. Everything we do for other humans, we should consider it *Sadaqah*. This is when the doors of *Barakah* (blessings) open.

This thought process instantly eliminates expectations and showing off. The moment we expect from a human, we bind ourselves in invisible chains. Let yourself free – free from desires – and you will see the world at your feet, taking in the air of freedom you never had the chance to breathe!

Crab Mentality

As a little girl, I was extremely passionate and possessive about my writing. I loved writing, and my favourite class was Urdu, where I would write my thoughts and ideas in the form of essays and articles, which were mostly part of my school homework. I carefully maintained my essay journal, and it was very close to my heart. I was a bright student and got the best grades. One day I opened my essay journal to find that the pages had some markings, which meant that someone had intruded my private space, gained access to my writings and copied my work. I felt very sad. Further to my shock, I found out it was my mother who had given my journal to her friend's son who needed some help. I cried the whole night, but this episode taught me two lessons:

- Knowledge is not to be kept hidden as a secret. It is meant to be shared for the benefit of others.
- I deserved a valued recognition for my work, leaving a legacy behind for others to take inspiration from.

I made spreading knowledge the purpose of my life, while at the same time it had woven a dream, a dream to become a published writer.

I started giving pieces of knowledge to the unseen bit by bit. As I did this, I realised I was gaining abundance in knowledge. Doors of wisdom and insights started opening for me. People had started treating me as a knowledge expert, and my worth had started increasing. The secret to abundance was unveiled to me in astonishing ways. I became abundant not only in knowledge but also in peace and happiness. I embarked on the journey of self-discovery and started feeling a sense of fulfilment in uplifting others through my wisdom and intellect.

'We rise by lifting others'
– Robert Ingersoll

What holds you back from uplifting others? They are your own insecurities. No one can take your limelight. A society cannot grow where its people suffer from crab mentality – a metaphor that refers to the pattern of the behaviour of crabs trapped in a bucket. While one crab can easily escape, its efforts will be undermined by others, ensuring the group's collective demise. It is a toxic mindset where people look for selfish gains and pull each other down instead of applauding the success of their peers.

If I can't have it, neither can you!

This results in a rotten and stagnant society where people remain stuck in their situation and no one reaches his potential. Out of envy, resentment, spite, conspiracy or competitive feelings, other people will halt your progress. The plight of such a society is miserable!

فرد قائم ربطِ ملت سے ہے، تنہا کچھ نہیں
موج ہے دریا میں اور بیرونِ دریا کچھ نہیں

The individual is firm by nation's coherence, otherwise nothing
The wave is only in the ocean, and outside it is nothing
– Allama Muhammad Iqbal

Great progress can be made when women uplift other women. They can become an unstoppable force and can build a tribe of empowered women contributing towards society's collective growth. In order for you to not become a miser in helping and supporting others, have the belief that your fate is prewritten and your share of wealth, fame and success have already been allotted to you. Then, you will not fear losing it on your way to share your God's gifts with others. No matter how much anyone desires your share, he cannot take it away from you. This will motivate you to let go of your fears and be a giver and supporter with an open heart.

Living on the Edge

Sometimes, from fear of the unknown, you tend to accumulate wealth so much so that the purpose of your life becomes to save as much as possible in order to have a secure future. In all this, you forget that the provisions you are saving are meant to be utilised for a beneficial cause and not accumulated for tough times. When you spend your provisions for a beneficial cause and learn to live on the edge, you become closer to Allah. You put complete trust in Him for your journey ahead, relying on His support.

Often, people do not give due share to the people it rightly belongs to. For example, the share of inheritance of sisters is usually waived off by manipulating their emotions. You might have increased your wealth on paper but from the Unseen, it is a call for scarcity in your life.

> *'The secret to abundance is in letting go which does not belong to you.'*

The experience of living on the edge makes you a risk taker, because you do not have much to lose. You learn to swim in deep waters, instead of playing safe all the time.

Summary

- Abundance that comes from the Unseen is beyond any measure.
- Attract abundance in your life by spending from your current provisions no matter how limited they are.
- Do small acts of kindness for others. This builds a community whose foundations are laid on the values of care and compassion.
- Uplift one another; don't be a miser in motivating someone. This can be the best act of kindness.

Chapter Twelve

Amplify Your Influence

Become Immortal

You do a lot of financial planning for your retirement so that you can spend the last years of your life in comfort and non-reliance. You do long-term investments that give you maximum and lasting returns so that when you retire from work you still have resources and a running income. The presupposition of the provision pot that lasts your lifetime somewhat releases from you the anxiety of continuously saving, and encourages you to live your present life to the fullest. Overcoming challenges to pursue your passions, not giving up hope and not being scared by the 'what ifs' are some of the gains of believing that you own a provision pot. When your mental space is free from this anxiety, it paves the way for a greater purpose in life.

Remember the bag of coins that were given to you on the island? How about maximising the gains from its spending? How about spending them so wisely that you enjoy the returns even when you have left that island for good? The presupposition that you can multiply your gains and receive them even when you have transitioned from this world motivates you to build a **legacy – the continued charity!**

'We all die. The goal isn't to live forever, the goal is to create something that will.'
– Chuck Palahniuk

Future Pacing – Maximise Your Potential

Now that you know the gains of building a good legacy, you should learn how to create one. In this world, you will be occupied by mundane tasks that are needed to fulfil the life essentials. Your car will need maintenance, your house will need repair, your job will require you to work long hours – staying focused each and every day will be a struggle for you. This means you will often lose sight of your legacy. So that you are less distracted by daily life and remain focused on building your legacy, it is important that you future pace yourself.

View your life on a timeline. If you see your life as a whole, you will assume that you have enough time to set goals and achieve them. Divide your life into chunks of one, five or ten years, and set both long and short-term goals; this will strengthen your vision and the purpose you wish to achieve. Not only this, it will build the optimum anxiety to meet your targets. Future pace yourself into different chunks of your life. It will give you perspectives that you can benefit from, before you actually hit that stage of your life. To squeeze your potential to the maximum, remember your death often!

Let me create an analogy with a school assessment paper. The paper is divided into sections, and each section is allotted a duration to complete it. This ensures that you don't waste time on something where it is not needed. Every second of your time in that assessment gets utilised in the best manner. If it did not have sections and a time limit, there are greater chances of you still working on the first section when time is up!

The Shepherd in You

If you have the skills to influence others, you possess the power to inspire people and have a crowd following you.

Some people are gifted with influence and persuasion naturally, and some people learn it as a need for survival. I learnt influencing and persuasion under very unique circumstances, which go back to my childhood. I was the only girl in my family; I had two brothers. Mixing with other girls my age, mostly my cousins, was a big challenge. I was surrounded by cousins from both my parents' sides. I had a trio of cousin sisters, which carried forward even after my marriage, when I was blessed with another trio of sisters-in-law. Sisterhood is a special bond. Sisters support and care for one another against all odds, and in this case, I was always the odd. My ideas, my thoughts and my mannerisms were always alien to them, while they shared the same outlook because they were raised by the same mother and in an identical environment. If I had to build associations, I had to blend in and adopt their ways in order to be labelled 'correct' according to their definition. My self-esteem would get hurt by validating and agreeing to their perceptions about things and situations, which at times may have been entirely opposite to the way I see the world. If one of my cousins and I would disagree during play, discussions or other activities, she had the other two to validate her stance, and I was the odd one out. Seeking validation became my prime desire, and my environment compelled me to please people in order to gain acceptance. However, it was more of a blessing than a curse to accept that I am the victim of my circumstances.

For a great portion of life, I was criticised for my individuality. In order to avoid the pain of being labelled as always wrong, my circumstances taught me how to influence and convince others. At that time, I seldom realised that I was under training to acquire an incredible power – the power to influence and to inspire. Being sister-less once upon a time had been my greatest weakness, which later became my greatest strength. During those tender years, I learnt empathy: how to see things from others' perspectives and how to understand different points of views without accepting them or giving up my own. I learnt how to agree to disagree and how to forgive others for their behaviours. It taught me impartiality and how to look beyond relationships. I inspired people towards questioning their choices, to look beyond their conditioning, not to fit in a box and to carve their own path.

Each of us carries an influence. Positive or negative is another question. What impact you leave on others is a big responsibility on your shoulders. The people who leave a positive impact on other people by inspiring them and benefit others in some way or the other are the good shepherds, and the world calls them leaders. They contribute to making this world a better place and are remembered for their powerful legacy.

Signs of a Good Leader

Imagine you are stuck in a traffic jam, and one person from the crowd comes out and manages the blockage. All of a sudden everyone starts following his directions, and the traffic is cleared. A leader is **responsible.**

Imagine you belong to a class of 100 students. Your class has an exam the following day, and nobody is prepared for it because there's an India-Pakistan Cricket match on the following day. Your teacher is quite particular and strict about studies. Nobody dares to speak up, but one person in the class stands up and on behalf of the whole class asks for a relaxation from the teacher, knowing that it can cost him to damage his reputation and be labelled as being non-serious. A leader is **daring**.

Imagine you live in a society where injustice is the norm. Those who have associations and a strong backing get their work done; those who cannot speak for themselves are sidelined. If you speak up in the face of adversity and stand up for what is right, not what is popular, if you stand up for those who can't and take a stand to help others, you are a leader. A leader challenges and confronts the status quo and **leads from the front** at the time of crisis.

The difference between a boss and a leader is that a boss controls while a leader gives ownership. A boss desires submission and practises authority, while a leader is just there to navigate the ship out of danger zones. He lets it sail freely otherwise. A leader understands his team very well; he possesses strong emotional and social intelligence. A boss wants you to fail so that he can lead you to success and take credit, while a leader does not hesitate to give credit when needed and keeps his team motivated. He works for a cause and not for self-promotion. A leader is one who creates more leaders, **leads from behind** during easier times, giving an opportunity to people to prove their mettle and helping them grow. This produces a set of individuals expert in their field, identifying their potential and putting them to good use.

> *'It is better to lead from behind and to put others in front, especially when you celebrate victory when nice things occur. You take the front line when there is danger. Then people will appreciate your leadership.'*
> *– Nelson Mandela*

While you will be leading from behind, there will be times when people won't be recognising your efforts and will try to let you down. Remember your Why. It should be big enough to snatch you out from the negative space or any drama that people may set up for you. Choose your battles wisely!

A leader is **accountable.** Being a leader comes with a big responsibility and can sometimes be a heavy burden to carry. As a leader, you carry not only the energy and consequences of your own actions but also of all those that follow suit. You are blessed with the potential, and hence you are tested accordingly. Are you using your power for the betterment of the people and this world, or you are using it for your own promotion and ego boost? Make a wise choice. You can easily lose focus and turn into a narcissist because of the thousands that follow you. Use your influence for a bigger purpose. Don't waste it in setting ordinary trends. Think big! Know your Why!

Have you experienced that people often imitate you? They can copy the way you dress, can go and buy things you own, things you do, places you go to – in short, they can copy you in every way possible! The good news is that people imitate you because you are a source of inspiration for them. You can utilise this power to become a change agent, but imitation can become a pain point when people copy your ideas without giving you credit. It can threaten your identity and become a source of annoyance when people start using it against you, giving rise to a conflict of interest.

For example, your colleague at your workplace copies your ideas often but in front of the management when it is time to give due credit, he either stays quiet or takes the credit for himself. This is a conflict of interest, and it can result in you losing an opportunity to be noticed and promoted for your skills. However, what meaning you give to his behaviour is all that matters. How about being an influence for a better cause. Always remember people can copy your ideas but they cannot copy your why! Sooner or later, you will overshadow him, and your abilities will no longer be secret. The behaviour of your colleague is a signal of his insecurity and acknowledgement of your creativity. Utilise your creativity and influence in becoming a reformer to bring about positive impact in society.

Further, always remember that the ultimate and foremost Creator is the Almighty. Knowledge and creativity are divinely rooted; we are just receivers, some more blessed than others.

Leaders have excellent emotional and social intelligence. There are people who have an ocean of knowledge but lack the intelligence and skill to use it. They do not realise that for a piece of advice to be effective and reach the hearts of the people, it needs to be relevant. A leader knows what to say when and when to stay silent.

In order for the shepherd in you to become an influential leader, you need to possess a positive outlook towards life. You should have a growth mindset and an attitude of continuous learning, irrespective of whom you learn from. A leader is intuitive in his approach and takes decisions carefully, analysing the situation from multiple perspectives. When you exercise emotional and social intelligence as a leader, you get to see things from a broader perspective and can make decisions in ambiguous and unpredictable situations using presumptions and empathy.

On the contrary, people with low emotional and social intelligence only understand things when they experience a situation themselves. They do not have the capacity to foresee things and cannot make decisions that incorporate the interests of others.

A leader knows how to efficiently delegate tasks and extract the best out of his team. He inspires patience in people, strengthens them to face failures with grace and learn from these setbacks as a means and a stepping stone towards success.

It is often the case that when you newly start to discover yourself by taking a journey within, you get so enthralled by its magic, you get excited and brag about the newly discovered you. You look down upon others because of their superficial lives. There are high chances that with every step of self-discovery, you may find that you cannot connect with the people and society you belong to, but this does not give you the right to disown your loved ones or become a hermit and start dwelling in a jungle. The challenge is to live among them and feel the rub. It will only make you shine brighter. Amplify your influence and help them in showing the depths of the inner world that you have seen, so as to build a powerful legacy.

Leaders are always in the limelight, and therefore, they easily attract envy. Use this negative energy for your benefit as discussed in Chapter 6. Moreover, glitter and glamour come as a by-product; a leader can easily get distracted by it and lose focus of his purpose. Therefore, it is necessary to keep revisiting and strengthening your vision so as not to lose its sight. Using your influence and power for a greater cause turns you into a legend. Reaching the peak and achieving the extraordinary is a praiseworthy act, but continuous praise and admiration by people can boost your ego and delude you into self-obsession. The balance between fostering self-esteem and suppressing your ego is the way towards unleashing ultimate success, which we are going to discover in the next chapter.

Summary

- Future-pace yourself so that you can focus on utilising your time efficiently.
- Discover your potential and use it to influence others, helping them to grow and take on a similar journey.
- Being a leader comes with a great responsibility; use your influence mindfully. This is the legacy that you will be leaving behind.
- Don't be deluded by self-obsession. Remain focused on building a powerful legacy. Utilise this temporary residence to maximise your gains that carry forward even after you die.

Chapter Thirteen

Unleash Success

You may become highly influential and inspirational, but in order to unleash ultimate success, adorn yourself with humility. It is a precious jewel that adds a sparkle to you inside and out.

Ego Attack

At your workplace, you may have noticed people who try to take credit for other people's efforts, usually their subordinates, and position themselves in a way that gives the impression that they were the ones who did all the work.

Your ego also comes into play in your relationships, where you want to be the one who is always right, and even if your partner is right, you try to undermine his point of view just to prove your supremacy. It requires a big heart to accept your mistake. When you become comfortable accepting your flaws and mistakes, you find it easy to forgive others for their shortcomings as well.

A child is the father of man. The toughest lessons of life have been the ones taught to me by observing my children as they grew up. But when parents see their children as reflections of themselves, rather than as separate individuals, it may be a manifestation of parental ego. At this point, the learning you acquire from them stops, and you influence them into being like you.

Ego also attacks you when you have more knowledge than others. Knowledge can sometimes be the source of an ego boost, giving you a feeling of superiority – that you are better than others. Scholars and people of knowledge, therefore, have to put extra efforts to keep themselves grounded.

When you consider yourself someone very important and high in rank, it becomes difficult for you to associate yourself with people lower in status than you. Negative feelings, such as anger, arrogance, resentment, fear and jealousy, are all products of the ego. Letting your ego go loose pushes you into the negative space. For you to stay on purpose, become productive and positive, you need to keep a check on your ego from time to time.

There can be many reasons for an ego attack: it could be difference in status, self-obsession, first impressions, background, neighbourhood, education, race, colour, creed – in short, any way in which you can relate yourself better than someone else.

Humility – Your Ultimate Success

Have you ever encountered a humble person in your life? What are the traits in his personality that stand out?

Humility is often mistaken for people-pleasing. It may seem as though a humble person submits to the wishes of others, but in fact, he is the master of his ego. Simplicity in his demeanour may give a false impression of being naïve, but his experiences and insights are the jewels that he wears and therefore he feels no need to boast or impress others by being a loud-mouth. A humble person's ego does not stop him in accepting failures; he is not shaken by setbacks, and he cannot fall into the pretence of being the perfect being as he submits to the Superior power accepting his limitedness and incapacity in front of the Almighty. He accepts himself with all his faults and mistakes. When you accept the wrong in you, only then there is a chance of bringing about a change within yourself.

When the ego stays hungry, you enter the world of self-discovery. The secrets of the universe are revealed to you. You start feeding your soul; you become real, genuine and authentic. You don't get stuck with the ills of materialism but are attracted to more substantial things that not only connect you with this world but also with eternal life. These connections are on deeper levels. You get to identify your Creator. You discover the purpose of your creation. You strive in achieving balance and peace. Being focused on your purpose and persistently working to achieve it gives you a sense of accomplishment. The journey starts with self-awareness and leads to God awareness; that is, it starts from knowing yourself and ends in knowing your Creator.

Staying humble and grounded also connects you with people belonging to all backgrounds. You do not look down upon people belonging to origins, cultures or religions different from yours. As a result, people feel secure, safe and comfortable in your presence. You do not challenge them but accept the way they are. Acceptance leads to mutual connection and paves the way for exchange of learning and wisdom. It is your humility that turns you into a spiritual being that spreads light without discrimination or judgement.

People start adoring you because of your compassion and down-to-earth attitude. It gives you an opportunity to empower people and bring ease into their lives. You become a change agent, a person of powerful influence. Being a source of benefit to the world energises your soul, and you are blessed with positivity, which increases the spiritual light. As you become habitual in your humble outlook, you are surrounded by the *Nur* (light) more and more. Your presence becomes blissful to others. You become an asset to society. People recognise you beyond your looks, your possessions and your associations. In short, you transcend!

Humility stops you from being spontaneous and helps you to exercise patience in your everyday life.

The Human Need for Inspiration

You are not the source of absolute knowledge. There is always someone better than you who has more knowledge than you, and someone more knowledgeable than him and the chain continues, connecting you with the divine source of wisdom. The moment you think you are the source of knowledge, you come under ego attack and start going downhill in your journey of enlightenment. When you think that only you can inspire others, and no one can inspire you, you become stagnant. You can never become self-sufficient, especially in knowledge.

Hence you should always be connected to people greater in wisdom than you to fill your cup of knowledge, while at the same time there should be an outlet from which the knowledge flows through you to people who are lesser than you. This will ensure that society is enlightened and progresses in intellectual growth.

Always remember the prime quality of an avid knowledge seeker is humility. If you cannot appreciate the source of your knowledge, whatever it might be – sometimes you learn from your child or student, from a person lesser in status than you, from a subordinate or competitor – your ego will compel you to undermine them and you take credit, but without humility you will hold a leaky cup of knowledge. That knowledge won't stay for long, and you will not be able to reap its fruits. It is, therefore, the quality of a humble person to respect his teachers, parents and even his children, big or small, rich or poor, black or white – no matter who they are; he is always appreciative and grateful for their contribution in his life. Therefore, humility leads to abundance of knowledge.

Do you remember a teacher that would get angry at you for asking questions and silence you for being irrelevant? Chances are he does not know the answer but does not want to admit it. If you don't know the answer, it is okay; it is a sign of greatness to accept your unawareness of a subject. You are considered more credible when you say you will learn and research and will get back on this later. You are not the All Knowing and the ultimate source of knowledge; you are a carrier and a seeker of knowledge yourself. This attitude fosters respect for you in others.

Humans tend to get inspired and follow. This is how we aspire to become more. As a human, you seek recognition and success. And whoever you see close to your definition of success and achievement, you aspire to be like him. This creates a need for role models in a society. Role models in society inspire its members to be ambitious, to dream and become more.

> *'He who cannot be a good follower cannot be a good leader.'*
> *– Aristotle*

The biggest tragedy for a society is to lose its role models. If the role models are mocked and not valued and praised, they lose their worth in the hearts of the people. When a society does not have good role models, the society – in search of inspiration – falls into the pit of creating one from the bad shepherds. The ideals of success and achievement get distorted and take new meaning. This leads to the corruption of that society.

The Power of Praise

We have a human tendency to believe that if someone is praised by a lot of people, he must be something big. For example, if you need eye surgery, which surgeon are you going to hire from the many out there, provided you have the resources? The one who is unheard of or the one who is widely known and appreciated for his work?

Or if you want to get a professional service, whom are you going to select? When you see someone with many Instagram followers or Facebook fans and most importantly good reviews about their business, it is human nature to start believing in the quality of their work. Sometimes, even if you don't like their quality of service, out of peer pressure and social conformity you hesitate in voicing your concerns.

Hence, the likes on Facebook and Instagram endorse this fact that if a person has a lot of followers and is liked by many, he must be a big shot. He tends to become a role model and an inspirational figure for many.

Continuous praise and following give authority, power and influence. That is how role models come into being.

But on what criteria someone is followed is important and can be overshadowed by the human limitation of getting influenced by marketing and positioning gimmicks. In this era of immense materialism, a human eye can be illusioned to believe in things that are far from real. In order not to fall for this illusion, you need to soak yourself in divine light to distinguish between the hoax and substance.

If we look at this from a spiritual perspective, in order for you to not lose your moral compass and ensure the divine light keeps spreading, you praise the inspirational figures so that their legacy becomes timeless and is forwarded through generations, transforming morally corrupt societies into civilised nations. For this very reason, Prophets are supposed to be praised, and blessings are sent to them. You endorse their legacy and follow their footsteps. Also, following someone who is recognised and praised as an inspiring figure by people of all generations gives you validation that you are following the right track.

For society to stay healthy and keep growing, we recognise them as our moral compass and keep aspiring to be like them. When you make fun of divine messengers, you work at your own destruction. You damage your ideals and values by mocking at their legacy. Having no divine light to follow, you seek inspiration elsewhere and go astray. Therefore, it is very crucial to preserve the sanctity and honour of your Prophets.

Word of mouth is the most powerful form of referral, because no one risks his credibility of giving valued advice and feedback unless he is making money otherwise.

I deliberately used the word role model as a basic need of a society and not inspiration because if you are inspired by someone, a time will come when you will reach his excellence and would bypass his greatness. There will be a competition amongst people trying to beat each other's greatness; then who decides who is at the top and whom to follow? When inspiration ends, you get stuck to aspire for more. How about this belief that a role model is a perfect human being whose level of excellence cannot be reached? All you can do is aspire to come as close to his level of excellence but not reach it. This will unleash the maximum potential in you, taking the best out of you in order to compete with your own self in improving to be the one closest to him as possible without overthrowing him and engaging the dispute of deciding who tops the list. This will keep you grounded and humble.

However, people's ego often comes into play and disrupts peace by claiming self-righteousness, even in deciding which group or sect is closest to perfection. This leads to intolerance and corruption in the land.

The 'Holier Than Thou' Attitude

Your ego thrives on the assumption that you are the most righteous person. The ideals and beliefs you hold are correct, and all others are transgressors.

This creates arrogance in you, and all your actions, despite being righteous, go to waste. The learning becomes limited because you completely shut your brain to any outside idea. In short, you become stagnant, which is a severe blow to your personal growth. There should always be room for an open discussion where people can share their thoughts and ideas. Not with the intention to boast their knowledge and supremacy over a topic but with the intention to improve their learning curve and strive for mutual growth.

Breaking Stereotypes

The human brain is wired for meaningful categorisation. This is how it processes and learns things by categorising things that are similar, picking up their general traits and putting them into one group. This is how it processes information in its surroundings; otherwise it would have to relearn every time it saw something. It will be too much work for the brain to do and will be very exhausting. For example, if you see a furry thing that has four legs and triangular ears, you will identify it as a cat. Next time you see something similar, your brain will instantly identify it as a cat without doing the same processing again and again.

Often, people try to fit you in a box and tag you with a label because of this limitation of the human brain. If you believe in the empowerment of women, they will tag you as a feminist; if you dress a certain way, you will be assumed to belong to a certain type of people with certain traits common to them; if you support a political party, people will assume you to be like the perception they hold of that party. No matter what, people will hurl labels and judgements at you. Also, there is a common perception that if you are not with them, then you are against them. If you deny this accusation, you are forced to fit in a group that is against them.

In this world, it is difficult for you to choose your identity on your own. Embrace your uniqueness and do not identify yourself with any brand. Because the fact of the matter is no one and no group is perfect. Belonging to one will mean that you not only endorse its goodness but also embrace its flaws. And this way, it will make you stagnant in your growth. When people stand united against injustice or in support of a cause, it does not necessarily mean they all are similar in all aspects of their being. Every person is unique in his own way.

A person's humility and integrity can be put to test in situations where they are wrong. If they find it difficult to accept their mistake, it means they are a victim of their ego. Sometimes criticising others feeds the ego, as it gives a sense of satisfaction that you are better and superior to the other. Hence in this relative world, comparisons and competitions can lead to an ego boost if they are not utilised for growth and have ego-boosting agendas. Failures give the best lesson of humility. Nothing can teach you humility better than facing failures.

There are times when we try to act humble in order to win praise from other people. This is the most dangerous form of showing off.

When you feed the ego, you remain deluded in this world, which is a temporary abode. Pride may obstruct your vision. Hence, you fail to identify the purpose of your existence and waste your unidentified, hidden potential, which could lead you to lead a meaningful life and leave behind a legacy.

This world only remembers those who are beneficial to others. Self-accomplishments may be a parameter for your personal fulfilment, but only those people can leave imprints on the sands of time who have done something valuable in their life that in some way or the other benefits humanity.

Humility – The Optimum Balance Between the Ego and Self-Esteem

Have you ever checked your ego levels when people praise you? It is very important not to be deluded by praise.

When you reach an epitome of success and achievement, your attitude defines your legacy. Attainment builds self-esteem and boosts confidence. It ensures that you keep on breaking barriers and excel in your endeavours. Excellence becomes second nature. High self-esteem also ensures that you hold tight to your stronger values, dreams and passions. You build your identity. But, if you go overboard and tilt to the other side, you can turn into a self-obsessed, deluded maniac who becomes arrogant. An arrogant person is self-centred and cannot look beyond his own success and achievement. This can block your potential and turn you into that hare who slept under the tree. Humility helps you maintain the optimum balance between self-esteem and ego by displaying gratitude.

A humble person gives the credit of his accomplishments to God and his bounties and blessings upon him. When you praise and thank the Almighty for all that you have in your life, your glory serves humanity and is displayed in your gentleness towards others. If you believe it just to be your own effort, it turns you into a narcissist who is overly obsessed with himself, and you become a nuisance to society.

Have you experienced a situation where you took help from someone and thanked him for his support, but this in return boosted his ego? He started thinking very highly of himself and later at some point in time signified his favours upon you. If you praise and thank people who support you in your endeavours or assist you when needed, they come under an ego attack. But if you, along with thanking them, wish them the blessings from the

Almighty as a compensation for their effort, it will instantly remind them of the fact that we all belong to Him, and whatever abilities we possess, it is a result of His blessings upon us.

Both these actions of praising and thanking the Almighty and wishing people His blessings as compensation for their assistance ensure that both the egos are under check.

'Humility weakens your ego and builds your self-esteem.'

There are two extremes among people. First, there are those who are so humble in their approach that they have this limiting belief that you are not supposed to praise yourself, an extension of which is to not appreciate your children or family members in front of others. Such people are spendthrifts when it comes to throwing self-criticism but misers in publicly appreciating themselves or their loved ones. Such people often have negative self-talk and see things very critically. They are obsessed with perfection and are never satisfied with their achievements. They remain unfulfilled throughout their life because no amount of success will ever be enough for them.

The second category of people is those who overdo praise and appreciation so much so that people are exhausted with their self-promotion. They won't miss any opportunity to compliment themselves, whether the praise is about their education, their background, their children, their neighbourhood or their tailor or barber or anything that is associated with them. Whenever anyone shares their experience, these people will somehow divert the conversation to their own experience, telling them how fabulous and amazing it had been, thus overshadowing the initial conversation! Many times, their claims would be highly exaggerated. Such people are low on self-esteem, and their behaviour is an attempt of seeking outside validation.

Always remember there is a very fine line between humility and people-pleasing. People might take you granted for your humility, but always remember humility is not for people; instead it is the manifestation of servitude towards God. You need to check your direction: if your humility is directed towards people, you are no more than a people pleaser, and it will land you into human slavery.

At times, out of modesty, you will find people who will downplay their abilities and portray themselves lesser than what they actually are. The balance lies between not showing off and being who you are. Remember your skills and abilities are a fact and not your assumption. They will shine no matter how much you conceal them. Be who you are and show your true self. If you downplay your first impression, your capabilities will become obvious sooner or later. But people will always compare you with the first impression you made. They treat you based on the first few interactions. If you have downplayed your abilities, they get a wrong impression and level themselves a little higher than you. They used to have an ego boost seeing you lesser than them, which is often evident in their conversations trying to impress you with knowledge, abilities or material possessions that they think are way beyond your comprehension or possession. They start believing that you are lesser in abilities than them. But once you break their perception, they feel as if you have outgrown them comparing with your first impression as the point from where they thought you had started. As a result, they become insecure and jealous when they see you outshine them.

In order to build self-esteem in children, parents often motivate their child by elevating his abilities over their own with comments such as 'you have solved this math problem even before I could,' or 'you run faster than me.' As we live in the world of relativity, when children see this comparison and praise, it boosts their self-esteem. Similarly, out of respect for the elderly who have lost their sharpness and alertness with age, you don't elevate yourself; instead you stay humble so that you do not cripple their self-esteem.

If you are surrounded by people who are victims of their complexes, they will feel elevated when you downplay yourself in front of them, just so that they can feel good. Remember, you are not their parent and neither they have aged. There is no need for you to fake. Instead, they need to overcome their complexes and insecurities, learn and grow rather than seek worth by being under the illusion that they are better than you. If you still do so, you not only hurt yourself by compromising your self-worth, but they too become stagnant and do not grow out of their helpless state.

Practising Humility

- **Break the ice.** Initiate in greeting people, and be the first one to break the ice. Give a smile walking out of the grocery store, play with the kids holding onto their mothers in the immigration queue, motivate the student sitting next to you on the bus who is studying for his exams. You might not know how powerful these small gestures may turn out, provided your eyes are away from your mobile screen and you have noticed them in your surroundings.

  Sometimes, you may find it difficult to initiate a conversation because of the hesitation that maybe people won't reciprocate in a similar way and they might give you the cold shoulder. Some may think it is cool to walk with your nose high in the air. They might believe that this attitude attracts more attention and increases their worth. Always remember the first one to greet is more beloved in the eyes of your Lord. Some people will look down on you, but who can humiliate you if the Lord of the heavens has promised your elevation?

- **Connect and Disconnect.** Sometimes, your ego and pride would be so high, you will find difficult to let them go. Having humility in your character can then become a big challenge. Soul-cleansing by spending some time in solitude can help. Disconnecting and dis-associating yourself from worldly things and self-reflection will help overcome pride and ego. However, balance is the key. This does not mean you have to spend your time in monasteries for the rest of your lives. Always respect your human needs and understand the fact that you are not self-sufficient and need food, sex, relations and so forth for sustenance. Killing your desires is another form on non-acceptance of self and lands you into similar troubles as giving in to too much of your desires.

  Reconnect with the world when you feel that your energies have balanced. You will have to keep swinging back and forth to reach the desired state of equilibrium in your life. This cycle will help you in contemplating and analysing your 'self' so that you always find your centre whenever you have lost your way.
- **Befriend the soil.** Spend some time in the morning doing gardening, sitting on the ground, playing with the sand, breathing in fresh air. Reflect upon your creation. You will begin to realise that there is a special bond between the two of you. It will give you pleasure and peace you won't find elsewhere. Reflect upon your death. You will realise you have found a friend whom you can embrace and wrap around when you lose all your energy. When this world no longer accepts you, you will be happily resting in the arms of your old friend. Not only this, it will teach you humility and will balance your energies, making you realise from dust you came and to dust you shall return.

'No pain is more than lack of peace and contentment and no pleasure is more than balance and fulfilment.'

Summary

- Be on guard; your ego can attack you in very subtle ways.
- Humility is the balance that keeps you in the centre and ensures you are not hanging on either side of the pendulum.
- Your humility can be tested by how you deal with people lesser than you in status or weaker than you in power.
- To build a powerful legacy, your life should be beneficial to humanity.
- Complying with society or submitting to your Lord – in choosing between the two, choose the second.

Epilogue

The Circle of Life

It is December 2019; and we are back again, this time with our children. The winter breeze is gently caressing the cheeks of my children as they excitedly climb the mountain of Light (*Jabal an-Nūr*). The sun has already set, and one can see the pilgrims making their way down. The rocks, the sand, the sky all are witness to the transformational journey that many have taken through this pathway.

Many of them like myself have come to know the fountain of timeless knowledge so that when life throws difficult questions at them, and they find themselves tangled with confusion and doubt, they exactly know which blessed drink can quench their thirst. Many have come to gain equilibrium and balance in their disoriented perceptions. All of them know, no matter how much they find themselves tilted to one side of the pendulum, this place has the gravity and a restoring pull that can bring them back to the centre. A place that can neutralize your polarities and bless you with a new beginning with every sunrise.

As the kids are heading up, I am praying for them. For them to seek their centre, to set their compass so that when they find themselves lost, they can align themselves in the direction of absolute truth. I pray that they are able to break the shackles of societal conditioning that threatens their freedom. Whenever they are challenged by relative morals, they have the ability to gauge them with divine wisdom. The wisdom that was sent to the unconditioned and unlettered Prophet.

As we make our way to the cave, a voice touches our ears. We turn our heads to see an old man. The melody in his voice is mesmerizing enough to make you go in a trance. The man passes by us and we all join him in chorus:

اَللَّهُمَّ صَلِّ عَلَى سَيِّدِنَا مُحَمَّدٍ النَّبِيِّ الأُمِّيِّ وَ عَلَى آلِهِ وَصَحْبِهِ وَ سَلِّمْ

(Allahumma salli alaa Sayyidina Muhammadinin Nabiyyil Ummiyyi Wa ʿala Aalihi wa Sahbihi wa Sallim.)

"O Allah bless Sayyidina Muhammad, the unlettered Prophet, and his family and companions and grant them best of peace."

Client Testimonials

'Humaira is not only an amazing life coach but was also able to give me a perspective and viewpoint that had never occurred to me in my whole life.

These perspectives helped me shift my perspective or vision and see things in a different light so I could make changes for better.

Humaira is sincere and committed to her work, and I would definitely recommend her to anyone seeking guidance or help, with realigning their perspective or path in life.

Thank you so much Humaira for all your help, and I hope you continue to help many more people like me.'

Aiesha Zafeer
HR and Recruitment Expert

'I began my sessions with Coach Humaira in hopes of learning how to organise my daily schedule to achieve some important, but non-urgent, life-long goals, but I unexpectedly got so much more than that! Not only has she helped me take active steps towards my goals but through her skill and the bag of techniques up her sleeve, she has also helped me discover and overcome root issues in my psyche, ultimately resulting in better relationships with my husband, parents and myself.

In addressing my core issues, a way was paved to conquer lesser obstacles and technicalities, and she helped me replace self-destructive habits with productive ones.

What I love about Coach Humaira is her positivity, warmth, attentiveness and professionalism. Her quick wit and intuition will not waste your time, and you can be sure she will offer practical resources and solutions with any dilemma. I've never seen someone so selflessly dedicated to helping others.'

Sufeyh Sabawi
Home Schooling Specialist

'Humaira helps you list down your objectives and guides you to work through them via discussion and exercises; she is a fantastic motivator that helps you move ahead and pushes you to be the better version of yourself. I highly recommend Humaira as a life coach to everyone that needs a confidence booster and perspective builder to get out of the vicious cycle of self-doubt.

She is super professional and is your best confidant.'

Zainab Hashim
HR Specialist

'Humaira is focused and organised. She is still able to touch and identify areas one needs help with at a very deep and personal level.

The deep-guided conversations and effective, mindful questions posed to think of areas in life one at times takes for granted and tasks provided to work and get to know oneself impart a deep, lasting impact that continuously leaves one wanting to know more about oneself and wanting to bring out the best.'

Shafinah Shamsher
Oil and Gas Economist

'She has helped me rediscover my passions and re-fuelled my desire to pursue my dreams. Her methods are simple, yet very effective; Humaira has been able to successfully extract and address the core underlying issues and has guided me confidently through those challenges by teaching me to see things through different perspectives.

I will always remember her words "We are limited by our own beliefs"; indeed once we break free, we can be unstoppable!'

Madiha Zeeshan
Co-Founder, The Babe Movement

www.ingramcontent.com/pod-product-compliance
Lightning Source LLC
Chambersburg PA
CBHW020322010526
44107CB00054B/1937